O9-AIG-323

everything
goes with
ice cream

s'more bar milkshake

EVERYTHING GOES WITH ICE CREAM

by Koralee Teichroeb

PRESS

PRESS

215 Historic 25th Street, Ogen Utah

© 2012 Jo Packham

First published in the United States of America in 2013 by
Quarry Books, a member of
Quayside Publishing Group
100 Cummings Center
Suite 406-L
Beverly, Massachusetts 01915-6101
Telephone: (978) 282-9590
Fax: (978) 283-2742
www.quarrybooks.com

10 9 8 7 6 5 4 3 2 1

ISBN: 978-1-59253-854-6

Senior Editor: Jo Packham
Production Manager: Brandy Shay
Copy Editor: Cynthia Levens
Art Director: Matt Shay
Photography: Koralee Teichroeb

Ice cream ...
who would have thought?

Who would have thought I would be writing a book on ice cream? Not me, though now that I think about it, ice cream has always been in my life. It was a permanent staple in my home growing up, thanks to my dear old dad who loved his ice cream. We always had an unlimited supply of butter pecan or maple walnut ice cream in our freezer.

Then I remember the day my parents told me we were buying a Dairy Queen. I was sure I had died and gone to ice cream heaven. During my teenage years, I was known as the girl who owned the Dairy Queen; everyone wanted to be my friend. I had free range to all the ice cream, sauces, and toppings a teenage girl could ever want. I would concoct blissfully wild and crazy ice cream treats for my friends. To this day I still remember my personal favorite: a gooey marshmallow pineapple vanilla milkshake topped with mounds of whipped cream and a cherry {or maybe 3 or 4}.

So with all my childhood ice cream exposure, I guess an ice cream book is the perfect fit for me ... I am even starting to wonder why I didn't think of it on my own. It took my dear friend Jo Packham, creator and editor-in-chief of Where Women Cook, to enthusiastically nudge me into this whole ice cream book notion. She was the one that came up with the idea of a book and had complete faith in me, so thank you Jo for this amazing ice cream adventure.

Plus, a big thank you hug goes out to my husband, daughters, and son-in-law who were my ice cream guinea pigs. I can honestly say they tested every single recipe in this book {our freezer was jam-packed with ice cream for months and months}. They have their own personal ice cream favorites, but I am not going to tell you which ones, as I am hoping you will find your own among the pages of this book.

Ice cream is a joy we can all experience. It's all about having fun, enjoying those special moments, not taking life too seriously, and totally forgetting about your diet just for a wee little bit.

Koralee Teichroeb

Contents

Scratch

{to make something from the very beginning; made from basic ingredients}

Nothing can compare to the taste of homemade ice cream made from only the freshest ingredients. Any time of the year can be homemade ice cream time; refreshing Summer Peach or Strawberry, cozy Autumn Pumpkin Pie, and festive Wintery Candy Cane. Remember nothing screams fun more than making up a batch of your own ice cream.

Vanilla Bean ice cream

Simple Vanilla Bean Ice Cream

This recipe is one you will use over and over again. Rich and creamy, it's perfect for experimenting with your own flavour combinations. Just stir in your favorite topping{s} after the ice cream has been made … it is that simple!

Makes 6 to 8 cups

1	vanilla bean pod
1½	cups whole milk
1¼	cups sugar
3	cups heavy cream
1	TB. vanilla extract

*No vanilla bean? No trouble, you can add 1 extra tablespoon vanilla extract.

1. Split vanilla bean pod in half; remove seeds by scraping inside pod with sharp knife.

2. In bowl, combine whole milk, sugar, and vanilla bean seeds; stir until sugar is dissolved.

3. Stir in heavy cream and vanilla extract.

4. Pour mixture into ice cream maker's freezer cylinder and follow manufacturer's instructions.

5. Within 30 minutes ice cream will be soft serve.

6. For firmer consistency, transfer ice cream into airtight freezer container and freeze for at least 2 more hours.

Homemade Sprinkles

Oh me oh my ... pure little bits of sugary joy! I just love sprinkles, so being able to make my own is pure heaven. Yes, you can do it too! Give it a go; you will be surprised how easy it is to spruce up your vanilla.

Or, add ½ cup store-bought sprinkles to ice cream while processing to create your own confetti ice cream! Happy decorating!

Makes 6 to 8 cups

> 1 cup icing sugar
> 1 TB. whole milk*
> 1 tsp. light corn syrup
> Liquid food coloring {1 color per batch}
> Piping bag/baggie with hole cut out of bottom

*I tried adding more milk, but the mixture was too runny. With less milk, it was too thick. After several tries I found that just a little more than 1 TB. milk worked perfectly.

1. In bowl, combine icing sugar, whole milk, and light corn syrup; stir until well-blended. {To make more than 1 color of sprinkles, divide mixture into batches.}
2. Add 1 color to each batch, a little bit at a time, until desired color is obtained.
3. Put 1 batch into piping bag.
4. Pipe little circles onto wax paper.
5. Repeat in new bags with additional batches.
6. Let dry overnight. Once hardened, sprinkles will pop off wax paper very easily.

Just for **today** ...
be **enthusiastic**
about the **success**
of **others** just as you
are about your **own**.

sprucing up
the
vanilla

Teacup Pincushion

Use enough batting to fill the teacup; make the batting into a ball, cover it with fabric {you will need to estimate the fabric circle size depending on the size of the teacup}, and secure tightly with elastic band. Cut off excess fabric, and make sure the fabric lays evenly around the ball {no puckers}. Pop covered ball into the teacup. It should fit securely without glue. I like having the option of reusing the teacup when it is time for a change.

Surprise a friend with a teacup pincushion

if you **love** *someone you better hurry up and show it*

Strawberry Ice Cream

This ice cream is best when made with fresh ripe berries, but frozen unsweetened berries can be substituted.

Makes 6 to 8 cups

- 3 cups fresh strawberries, sliced
- 3½ TB. fresh lemon juice
- 1½ cups sugar
- 1¼ cups whole milk
- 2¾ cups heavy cream
- 2 tsp. vanilla extract

1. In bowl, combine fresh strawberries, fresh lemon juice, and ½ cup sugar. Let sit at least 1½ hours.

2. Strain strawberries, saving juice. Mash half of strawberries, but save rest.

3. In separate bowl, combine whole milk and remaining 1 cup sugar; stir until sugar is dissolved.

4. Stir in heavy cream, mashed strawberries, reserved juices, and vanilla extract.

5. Pour mixture into ice cream maker's freezer cylinder and follow manufacturer's instructions.

6. Within 30 minutes ice cream will be soft serve. Add reserved sliced strawberries to cylinder and process another few minutes until well-blended.

7. For firmer consistency, transfer ice cream into airtight freezer container and freeze at least 2 more hours.

Blooming Teacups

There is nothing like the joy of having tiny spring flowers blooming from a darling teacup in the midst of winter. Plant several to line a window ledge … they make waiting for spring a lot easier.

You'll need a few teacups, soil, bulbs {I like grape hyacinths or narcissus; tiny bulbs work best for the small cups}, and small pebbles.

Place enough pebbles in the bottom of the cups for drainage; top with soil and place bulbs on top {I find 3 bulbs are perfect for these tiny cups}. Make sure to put the root end of the bulbs down on top of the soil. Sprinkle with more pebbles; water well, but do not overwater or bulbs will rot. The bulbs should be just sitting on top of the soil.

Place in a cool, dark place until roots start to grow {mine only took 6 days, but they could take up to 10 days or more}. Continue to water. Once roots take hold, bring into a warm sunny room; water and watch as your bulbs start to sprout and grow.

do not wish to be anything else but what you are

Peach Cream Ice Cream

Nothing reminds me of summer more than plump juicy peaches picked fresh from an orchard tree. The flavour of sweet peaches mixed with rich cream is heavenly. Remember: Only the ripest, sweetest peaches will do!

Makes 6 to 8 cups

3	cups fresh peaches, sliced
3½	TB. fresh lemon juice
1½	cups sugar
1¼	cups whole milk
2¾	cups heavy cream
2	tsp. vanilla extract

1. In bowl, combine fresh peaches, fresh lemon juice, and ½ cup sugar. Let sit at least 1½ hours.

2. Strain peaches, saving juice. Mash half of peaches, but save rest.

3. In separate bowl, combine whole milk and remaining 1 cup sugar; stir until sugar is dissolved.

4. Stir in heavy cream, mashed peaches, reserved juices, and vanilla extract.

5. Pour mixture into ice cream maker's freezer cylinder and follow manufacturer's instructions.

6. Within 30 minutes ice cream will be soft serve. Add reserved sliced peaches to cylinder and process another few minutes until well-blended.

7. For firmer consistency, transfer ice cream into airtight freezer container and freeze at least 2 more hours.

Pink Marshmallow Ice Cream

Mini pink marshmallows along with fluffy marshmallow creme makes this pretty pink ice cream delightfully sweet.

Makes 6 to 8 cups

- 1½ cups whole milk
- 1½ cups sugar
- 3 cups heavy cream
- 2 TB. vanilla extract
- Pink gel food coloring
- 1 cup marshmallow creme
- 1 cup pink mini marshmallows (sorted out from a bag of colored marshmallows if you can't find only pink)

1. In bowl, combine whole milk and sugar; stir until sugar is dissolved.

2. Stir in heavy cream and vanilla extract.

3. Pour mixture into ice cream maker's freezer cylinder and follow manufacturer's instructions. Add pink food coloring while mixing, just a bit at a time until desired color is obtained.

4. Ice cream should be done within 25–30 minutes. Add marshmallow creme and continue to blend. The marshmallow creme will get very hard when cold, so blend until well-mixed or leave little chunks for texture. {I like to have a white marshmallow ribbon running through my ice cream.} Add mini marshmallows; combine well.

5. For firmer consistency, transfer ice cream into airtight freezer container and freeze at least 2 more hours.

Pink Marshmallow Sticks

In my book, nothing is sweeter than fluffy pink marshmallows. So why not double this sweetness by pairing Pink Marshmallow Ice Cream with these homemade graham cracker shortbread sticks covered with more pink marshmallows?

Ooh la la!

Makes 15 sticks

6	TB. butter
¼	cup brown sugar
1½	tsp. vanilla extract
½	tsp. cinnamon
	Pinch of salt
⅔	cup flour
¼	cup graham cracker crumbs
½–¾	cup mini pink marshmallows

1. Preheat oven to 375°F.

2. Melt butter in saucepan. Remove from heat and stir in brown sugar, vanilla extract, cinnamon, and salt. Stir in flour and graham cracker crumbs. Mixture should be crumbly.

3. Press crumb mixture into bottom of 8" x 8" baking dish. Bake until firm, about 10–12 minutes.

4. Preheat broiler. Spread mini pink marshmallows evenly over baked crumb mixture. Broil until marshmallows are slightly melted and golden brown on top. Watch closely as they will burn quickly; 50 seconds should do. Remove and let cool slightly before cutting.

pink marshmallow sticks

Blueberry *Coconut ice milk*

Meet Molly, Daughter Number 2

Molly is my middle child. She is my free-spirited vegetarian, here today/gone tomorrow, let's-travel-the-world-and-worry about-things-later daughter.

Blueberries and coconut are two of her favorite things. They blend nicely together to create a lighter but very favourable ice milk. Being who she is, crunchy granola is the perfect way to top her ice milk treat.

Molly's Blueberry Coconut Ice Milk

Makes 6 cups

> 3 cups coconut milk
> 2½ cups blueberries, fresh/frozen
> 4 TB. honey
> 1 tsp. vanilla extract

1. In blender, mix together coconut milk, fresh or frozen blueberries, honey, and vanilla extract until smooth.

2. Transfer to bowl, cover, and refrigerate 1 hour.

3. Pour mixture into ice cream maker's freezer cylinder and follow manufacturer's instructions.

4. Within 30 minutes ice cream will be soft serve.

5. For firmer consistency, transfer ice cream into airtight freezer container and freeze at least 2 more hours.

6. Top with Molly's Crunchy Granola.

Molly's Crunchy Granola

Makes 6 to 8 cups

3	cups quick-rolled oats
1	heaping cup almonds, slivered
1	cup unsweetened coconut, shredded
1	tsp. cinnamon
½	cup butter
½	cup honey
⅔	cup brown sugar
	Splash of vanilla extract
	Parchment paper

1. Preheat oven to 350°F.

2. In large bowl, combine quick-rolled oats, almonds, unsweetened coconut, and cinnamon.

3. In saucepan, melt butter. Add honey and brown sugar; stir until sugar is dissolved. Remove from heat and stir in vanilla extract.

4. Pour butter mixture over oat mixture; stir until oats are well-coated.

5. Spread evenly onto cookie sheet covered with parchment paper.

6. Bake 30 minutes, stirring every 10 minutes.

7. Let cool before transferring to sealed container to store.

Pumpkin Pie Ice Cream

This is my all-time favorite; as close to pumpkin pie as you will get.

Makes 6 to 8 cups

- 1½ cups whole milk
- 1 cup brown sugar
- 2 TB. molasses
- 1¾ cups canned pumpkin purée
- 2 tsp. cinnamon
- 1 tsp. ginger
- ¼ tsp. nutmeg
- 2½ cups heavy cream
- 1½ tsp. vanilla extract
- Pumpkin seeds, roasted & salted {optional}

1. In bowl, combine whole milk, brown sugar, and molasses; stir until well-mixed.

2. Stir in canned pumpkin purée, cinnamon, ginger, and nutmeg.

3. Stir in heavy cream and vanilla extract.

4. Pour mixture into ice cream maker's freezer cylinder and follow manufacturer's instructions.

5. Within 30 minutes ice cream will be soft serve.

6. For firmer consistency, transfer ice cream into airtight freezer container and freeze at least 2 more hours.

OPTIONAL: For extra crunch, top with roasted, salted pumpkin seeds when serving!

Just for today ... find a smile among the familiar.

Praline Ice Cream

Crunchy toasted pecans covered with a sweet caramelized topping.

Makes 6 to 8 cups

PRALINE

¾ cup sugar

¼ cup water

1 cup whole pecans

1 TB. butter

ICE CREAM

1½ cups whole milk

1¼ cups sugar

3 cups heavy cream

2 TB. vanilla extract

PRALINE

1. Spray baking sheet with nonstick cooking spray. Combine sugar and water in small saucepan and place over medium heat; cook until sugar dissolves. Increase heat to high and cook until mixture is amber in color.

2. Remove from heat and stir in whole pecans and butter.

3. Pour pecan mixture onto prepared baking sheet and let cool completely. Once cool, break into small pieces.

ICE CREAM

1. In bowl, combine whole milk and sugar; stir until sugar is dissolved.

2. Stir in heavy cream and vanilla extract.

3. Pour mixture into ice cream maker's freezer cylinder and follow manufacturer's instructions.

4. Within 30 minutes ice cream will be soft serve. Add praline to ice cream mixture and let process until well-blended.

5. For firmer consistency, transfer ice cream into airtight freezer container and freeze at least 2 more hours.

Praline
ice cream

Double Chocolate Ice Cream

Very rich and decadent. If you are a chocolate lover, this is the ice cream for you.

Makes 6 to 8 cups

- ⅔ cup sugar
- ½ cup brown sugar
- 1 cup unsweetened cocoa powder
- 1½ cups whole milk
- 3 cups heavy cream
- 1½ TB. vanilla extract
- 1 cup good quality dark chocolate, chopped

1. In bowl, combine sugar, brown sugar, and unsweetened cocoa powder. Add whole milk and stir until sugars are dissolved.

2. Stir in heavy cream and vanilla extract.

3. Pour mixture into ice cream maker's freezer cylinder and follow manufacturer's instructions.

4. Within 30 minutes ice cream will be soft serve. Add dark chocolate and continue to process until well-blended.

5. For firmer consistency, transfer ice cream into airtight freezer container and freeze at least 2 more hours.

Double Chocolate ice cream

Coffee Ice Cream

Coffee lovers everywhere will adore this rich ice cream filled with thin and crunchy dark chocolate pieces.

Makes 6 to 8 cups

- 1½ cups whole milk
- ¾ cup sugar
- ⅓ cup brown sugar
- 2 TB. instant coffee
- 3 cups heavy cream
- 1½ tsp. vanilla extract
- 1 cup dark chocolate, tempered & chopped (see recipe on page 79)

1. In bowl, combine whole milk, sugar, brown sugar, and instant coffee; stir until coffee and sugar are completely dissolved.

2. Stir in heavy cream and vanilla extract.

3. Pour mixture into ice cream maker's freezer cylinder and follow manufacturer's instructions.

4. Within 30 minutes ice cream will be soft serve. Add dark chocolate and continue to process until well-blended.

5. For firmer consistency, transfer ice cream into airtight freezer container and freeze at least 2 more hours.

Just for today ... give yourself a little bit of your own attention.

Red Velvet Ice Cream

All three of my girls, as well as my son-in-law, voted this recipe as their all-time favorite homemade ice cream. It is delicious … cream cheese, red velvet cake, and cocoa mixed into freshly churned vanilla ice cream. The beautiful colors that the red cake and cocoa swirls produce are a bonus; it really is a very pretty ice cream.

Makes one 9x13-inch cake or two 9-inch rounds

RED VELVET CAKE

- 2½ cups flour, sifted
- ½ tsp. salt
- 2 TB. plus ½ tsp. unsweetened cocoa powder, sifted
- 2 TB. red liquid food coloring
- 1 cup buttermilk
- ½ cup butter, room temperature
- 1½ cups sugar
- 2 tsp. vanilla extract
- 2 eggs
- 1 tsp. baking soda
- 1 tsp. white vinegar
- Parchment paper

1. Preheat oven to 350ºF Spray cake pan{s} with nonstick cooking spray and line with parchment paper.

2. Sift together flour, salt, and unsweetened cocoa powder; set aside.

3. Mix red food coloring into buttermilk; set aside.

4. Beat butter until smooth. Add sugar, vanilla extract, and eggs one at a time.

5. Alternate adding buttermilk mixture and flour mixture to butter mixture. Beat well after each addition.

6. Mix baking soda into white vinegar and, while still foamy, hand stir immediately into batter.

7. Pour batter into prepared pan{s}. Bake 25 minutes or until top springs back when touched. Let cool completely before cutting.

NOTE: Only 2 cups of this cake are needed for the Red Velvet Ice Cream, so you will have lots left over to enjoy!

Just for today ...
keep your promises.

Makes 6 to 8 cups

RED VELVET ICE CREAM

    2 cups Red Velvet Cake, cubed

 1¼ cups whole milk

 1½ cups sugar

    1 {8 oz.} packet cream cheese, softened & cubed

    3 cups heavy cream

    2 tsp. vanilla extract

    1 TB. unsweetened cocoa powder, sifted

    1 TB. red liquid food coloring

1. Put Red Velvet Cake in freezer to firm for adding to ice cream mixture later.

2. In bowl, beat whole milk, sugar, and cream cheese until well-blended {not all cream cheese pieces will blend evenly, but that is fine; there should be some small cream cheese pieces in finished ice cream. Just make sure there aren't any big chunks}.

3. Stir in heavy cream and vanilla extract; blend well.

4. Pour mixture into ice cream maker's freezer cylinder and follow manufacturer's directions. Process about 25–30 minutes.

5. While processing, mix together unsweetened cocoa powder and red food coloring. Make sure they are blended well to avoid chunks of red food coloring in ice cream.

6. Once ice cream is complete, add frozen cake pieces; process for 1 minute until well-incorporated.

7. Add cocoa mixture; process until ribbons of reddish brown begin to form in ice cream.

NOTE: Be careful not to mix cocoa completely or ice cream will turn pink. Ice cream should remain white with reddish brown swirls. This can be tricky as cocoa mixture should mix in just enough to avoid biting into bitter cocoa powder. Once mixed, soft serve is ready to eat.

8. For firmer consistency, transfer ice cream into airtight freezer container and freeze at least 2 more hours.

A wee little tea light charmer

Teacup Candles

These are so easy to make. Perfect for gift giving and a great way to recycle old candles.

- Old candles {same color}
- Double boiler for melting wax {this pan may not be used for food preparation after it has been used to melt wax}
- Wick & wick sustainers {you can purchase these attached together}
- Long skewer/fork handle to wrap wick around while wax is drying
- Pretty teacups {sugar bowls work nicely as well}

1. Cut old candles into small pieces for easy melting. Remove wicks before putting candles into double boiler.

NOTE: The number of old candles needed depends on number and size of teacups. You will need to estimate. Melt a few candles, pour into cup, and repeat if necessary.

2. Place double boiler over medium heat {an electric burner is safer for this process}. Melt wax.

3. Gently wrap wick around small skewer or fork handle. Dip sustainer into melted wax, and stick wick with sustainer onto bottom of teacup, adhering it to bottom center of teacup. Press firmly. Lay skewer or fork handle over top of teacup's rim, making sure wick is straight.

4. Carefully pour melted wax into prepared teacup, trying to keep wick as straight as possible. Leave ½-inch rim around top of teacup.

5. Let wax set. A well may form once wax sets; just add more melted wax to even top out.

6. Once wax is completely set, cut wick to desired size.

Just for today ...
remember joy is what you are.

Candy Cane ice cream

Candy Cane Ice Cream

So perfect for a wintery treat. For a festive twist, add one spoonful of this ice cream to hot cocoa.

Makes 6 to 8 cups

8	candy canes
1½	cups whole milk
1¼	cups sugar
3	cups heavy cream
1½	TB. vanilla extract

1. Unwrap candy canes and crush finely in food processor.

2. In bowl, combine whole milk and sugar; stir until sugar is dissolved.

3. Stir in heavy cream and vanilla extract.

4. Pour mixture into ice cream maker's freezer cylinder and follow manufacturer's instructions.

5. Within 30 minutes ice cream will be soft serve. Add crushed candy canes into cylinder and continue to process for a few minutes until well-blended.

6. For firmer consistency, transfer ice cream into airtight freezer container and freeze at least more 2 hours.

there is candy cane ice cream in my
hot cocoa

flirty floral
hang
stack
adore

will you hold my
baubles &
beads

the
thrill
of
the
hunt

Just for today ...
discover your
gifts and **use**
them **wisely.**

Saucer Treat Stand

Make these in no time. A perfect way to display your sweet treats.

All you will need are little odd saucers, candle sticks, egg cups, or little vases for the bases; and clear epoxy craft glue.

Clean and dry dishes thoroughly. Find the center of the saucer. Glue the base onto the bottom of the saucer. Let glue dry completely before using.

Hand wipe the saucer after each use; do not put it in the dishwasher.

simply
divine
treat
stand

Festive
{Watering the Flowers}

Welcome blue skies and sunshiny festive days with these blissfully delightful treats.

it's a raspberry kind of day

Ice Cream Bombes

Easy to make but oh so elegant to look at. With just a few simple ingredients you can make these beautiful desserts in a snap. It is important to freeze each layer well before adding another.

Raspberry Bombe

Makes 6 to 8 servings

Ingredient amounts will depend on mould size.

- 1 cup fresh raspberries, enough to line bottom of bowl, plus extra for garnish
- 1½ cups vanilla ice cream
- 1 cup raspberry sorbet
- 4 cup metal mixing bowl

1. Chill 2 regular mixing bowls in freezer.

2. Line metal mixing bowl with plastic wrap, leaving edges overhanging. Place lined bowl in freezer for 10-15 minutes.

3. Wash and dry fresh raspberries really well. Adding raspberries 1 by 1, place each face up {stem side down} so there is a single layer of raspberries lining bottom and sides of metal bowl. Place in freezer for 15-20 minutes.

4. Place vanilla ice cream in 1 chilled mixing bowl. Beat on low speed until ice cream is spreadable, about 20-30 seconds. Remove chilled mould lined with raspberries from freezer. Fill raspberry bowl ¾ full with ice cream. Smooth top with spatula. Return mould to freezer for 30 minutes.

5. Place raspberry sorbet in second chilled mixing bowl. Beat on low speed until spreadable, about 30 seconds. Remove mould from freezer. Add layer of sorbet flush with rim of mould. Smooth top, cover with plastic wrap, and return to freezer until completely hardened, about 5 hours or overnight.

6. See Removing Bombes from Moulds.

Blueberry Bombe

This bombe is made the same way as the Raspberry Bombe, but layered differently. That is the beauty of these bombes: You can be creative and layer as many times as you want with any flavour of ice cream, sorbet, or fruit.

Makes 6 to 8 servings

Ingredient amounts will depend on mould size.

- 2 cups blueberry sorbet
- 1 cup vanilla ice cream
- ¾ cup fresh blueberries
- 1 cup raspberry sorbet

1. Follow the directions for Raspberry Bombe noting different layer order below.

    *The first layer is blueberry sorbet.

    *The next layer is vanilla ice cream.

    *Add fresh blueberries to center and cover with layer of raspberry sorbet.

REMOVE BOMBES FROM MOULDS

To serve the bombe, place a serving plate upside down on top of the mould. Holding a plate against the mould, invert both. Place a hot, wet kitchen towel over the mould. The metal bowl should lift right off the bombe. Remove plastic wrap. Serve immediately; garnish with handful of fresh berries.

For easy slicing, let bombe sit a few minutes to soften. The bombe may have some defects, but as ice cream softens, smooth these areas with a spatula.

blueberry
bombe
{happy dance}

if one is *good.*

.... two is *Better*

Pom-Pom Garland

- Pom-pom maker {found in any craft store}
- Bits of fabric
- Yarn, a few different colors

1. Make pom-poms following pom-pom maker's instructions. Amount depends on desired length of garland and spacing of pom-poms. Make sure to leave a string on each of the pom-poms; this will help attach it to the garland.

2. Tear strips of fabric for ribbon.

3. Cut piece of yarn to desired length of garland. Start tying pom-poms and fabric strips onto yarn piece — the more random, the better. Let pom-pom ties hang down to create a fun, whimsical look.

Heartfelt Button Covers

Using a heart template, cut hearts out of a piece of felt fabric. With scissors, make a slit in the middle of each heart big enough to fit over the shirt buttons. Button up shirt and slip hearts over tops of buttons. How cute is this?

buttons + hearts = sweetness

coconut ice

Coconut Ice

Coconut Ice is usually two-tiered and pink and white. It looks adorable packaged in clear cello bags to give away, or put on a pretty platter and added to your table for a festive celebration of any kind.

Makes 30 pieces

8	cups icing sugar, sifted, plus extra
2½	cups condensed milk
6	cups desiccated coconut, & shredded
1½	tsp. vanilla extract
	Pink gel food coloring
	White nonpareils sprinkles {or color of choice}
	Parchment paper

DESICCATED COCONUT

1. Preheat oven to 250°F. Spread a thin layer of shredded coconut onto a baking sheet as evenly as possible, avoiding any clumps so that the coconut will dry evenly. Bake coconut for about 5-10 minutes, checking frequently. Once coconut is completely dried, it will be brittle to the touch instead of soft. Remove from oven and let cool.

NOTE: Desiccated coconut is coconut meat that has been shredded or flaked and then dried to remove as much moisture as possible.

1. Place icing sugar, condensed milk, desiccated coconut, and vanilla extract into large bowl. Mix well.

NOTE: Using hands to mix dough works best, as mixture is very stiff.

2. Turn mixture onto surface lightly dusted with icing sugar and knead gently.

3. Divide mixture into 2 portions. Knead very small amount of pink food coloring into half of mixture until well-blended. Add more color if needed to reach desired shade.

4. Cover bottom of 9" x 11" baking tin with lightly greased parchment paper. Press non-colored half of mixture into bottom of baking dish. The dough dries out very fast, so smooth down edges and corners as quickly as you can.

NOTE: I used a small drinking glass as a rolling pin to get the top as flat and even as I could.

5. Place pink dough in bunches on top of non-colored dough and roll out as smooth as you can over top of white half. There should now be 2 even layers.

6. If desired, cover top with nonpareil sprinkles.

NOTE: Sprinkles do not like to stick, so they must be pressed down into dough.

7. Cover and refrigerate overnight to set.

8. Cut into finger- or bite-sized pieces. They are much easier to cut at room temperature once set; the cut pieces have smoother edges and are less likely to crumble.

9. Store in refrigerator up to 2 weeks. Best served at room temperature.

just a spoonful of sprinkles

Ice Cream Roll-Up Cake

Makes 8 servings

CAKE

- 4 eggs
- ¾ cup sugar
- 1¼ TB. oil
- 2 TB. buttermilk
- 1½ tsp. vanilla extract
- 1 tsp. cider vinegar
- Rose gel food coloring
- 1 cup flour
- 1 tsp. baking powder
- ½ tsp. salt
- Icing sugar, sifted
- Jellyroll pan/deep cookie sheet
- Parchment paper

1. Preheat oven to 350°F. Grease 9" x 13" jellyroll pan or deep cookie sheet and line with parchment paper. Grease parchment paper.

2. In large bowl, beat eggs until light in color, about 5 minutes.

3. Slowly mix sugar and oil into beaten eggs. Add buttermilk, vanilla extract, and cider vinegar.

4. Add drops of rose food coloring until desired shade is achieved.

5. Sift together flour, baking powder, and salt. Add to liquid ingredients in batches, mixing well after each batch, until all is well-combined.

6. Pour batter into greased pan, making sure batter covers entire pan.

7. Bake 12–15 minutes. Check often so it does not over-bake. Cake is done when it springs back when pressed with fingers.

8. While cake is baking, lightly cover large cotton tea towel with icing sugar. Rub icing sugar into towel so it is completely covered.

9. When cake is done, turn it out onto sugar-covered tea towel; cake should flip right out when quickly turned upside down. Peel off parchment and immediately roll tightly into the tea towel, beginning at the narrow end. Place rolled cake on wire rack seam-side down and let cool completely.

roll it on up

STRAWBERRY ICE CREAM FILLING

1½ cups fresh strawberries, puréed; plus sliced strawberries for garnish

2 cups vanilla ice cream, softened for easy spreading

Whipped cream

1. Once Cake is completely cooled, unroll. It's OK if it curls a bit; don't want to fight with it, as it can tear easily.

2. Gently fold fresh strawberries into ice cream.

4. Working quickly, spread ice cream mixture gently over entire cake. Once complete, start rolling cake up tightly, starting with the same end rolled up first before.

5. Cover with plastic wrap, and return to freezer until frozen solid, or overnight.

6. To serve, remove plastic wrap and slice with serrated knife. Garnish with sliced strawberries and whipped cream; serve immediately.

Roll-Up Cake with Butter Cream Frosting

Make cake according to instructions, but fill with a butter-cream icing instead of ice cream. To change the look, add any color of food coloring to the batter.

Pink Cinnamon Buns

Turn your everyday cinnamon buns into something festive and fun by adding a bit of pink food coloring to your dough. These are a great way to wake up a sleepy bunch of slumber party girls or add a cheery twist to a Mother's Day brunch. Or how about a baby shower treat: pink for a girl, blue for a boy?

Makes 12 buns

DOUGH

2	tsp. sugar, plus 6 TB.
1	cup lukewarm water
2	packages fast-rising dry yeast
2	cups whole milk
4	tsp. salt
¼	cup butter/margarine/shortening
1	cup cold water
10	cups flour
	Pink gel food coloring {for pink-colored buns}
½	cup butter, melted
1	cup brown sugar
1	TB. cinnamon

1. Add 2 teaspoons sugar to lukewarm water, stir, and sprinkle with fast-rising dry yeast. Let stand 10 minutes. Stir until blended.

2. Heat whole milk to almost boiling point. Stir in salt; 6 tablespoons sugar; butter, margarine, or shortening; and cold water. Let cool until lukewarm.

Just for today ... treat yourself to a small joy.

3. Stir milk mixture and yeast mixture together. Add 5 cups flour and work until all flour is well-blended. Mix pink food coloring into dough to reach desired shade. Make sure it is well-blended; but, not to worry if it is not because once dough is turned out on the table, kneading will blend the food coloring nicely.

4. Gradually add remainder of flour {may not need it all or may need a little more}. Turn out onto a greased tabletop and knead until smooth and elastic, about 8 minutes.

5. Place dough in lightly greased warm bowl. Grease top, and cover with cloth. Let rise in a warm place until double in size, about 1–1½ hours.

6. Preheat oven to 375°F.

7. Punch down dough and turn out onto greased tabletop. Roll out into rectangle. Rub top with melted butter, leaving ½" boarder uncovered, and sprinkle with brown sugar and cinnamon. Roll up dough. Cut into slices about ½" thick. Place into greased pans and let rise for about 1 hour or until double in size.

8. Bake at 375°F. for 25–30 minutes or until buns are golden brown.

9. Frost with Cream Cheese Icing.

Cream Cheese Icing

Frosts 12 buns

   ½ cup butter, room temperature

   1 {8 oz.} package cream cheese, room temperature

   1½ tsp. vanilla extract

   2–3 cups icing sugar

1. Mix butter and cream cheese together until smooth.

2. Add vanilla extract and icing sugar. Continue adding sugar until achieving desired sweetness and thickness.

we are all eligible for life's small pleasures

Heart-Shaped Meringue Cookies

Makes 24 to 30 cookies

- 3 egg whites
- ¼ tsp. cream of tartar
- ¾ cup sugar
- ¼ tsp. salt
- Pink gel food coloring
- White nonpareil sprinkles
- Parchment paper
- Heart-shaped cookie cutter
- Piping bag/baggie with hole cut out of bottom

1. Preheat oven to 200°F. Line baking tray with parchment paper.

2. Beat egg whites with electric mixer on medium speed until foamy.

3. Add cream of tartar, and continue beating egg whites. Add sugar and salt, a bit at a time and beating after each addition, until well-blended. Continue mixing until egg whites are stiff and glossy, about 5 minutes.

4. Add a few drops pink food coloring, mixing until desired shade is reached. Not much is needed.

5. Using heart-shaped cookie cutter, trace hearts onto parchment paper that is lining baking sheet. Fill piping bag with meringue, and pipe meringue over hearts to achieve heart-shaped cookies.

6. Bake 1½ hours. Turn off oven, but leave meringues in oven another 1½–2 hours or overnight, until completely cool. Store in airtight container.

NOTE: Serve Heart-Shaped Meringue Cookies with ice cream. Save broken pieces to add to ice cream sundaes. If you don't want to make heart-shaped cookies, just pipe out individual little puffed round ones.

Ice Cream Sundaes with Pink Meringue Pieces

The meringue pieces add a fun crunch to these sweet sundaes. You will need 1 or 2 Heart-Shaped Meringue Cookies for each sundae. Mix vanilla ice cream with broken pieces of cookies. Layer sundae with raspberries and ice cream and top with fruit and sprinkles.

Just for today ... wink at someone you love.

sprucing up the vanilla

Meet My Friend Amy

Amy Powers has been making things her whole life. As a young girl, she discovered the joy of escaping inward to the imaginative world of creativity. These days, she's cultivating her crafty skills, and sharing her creations on her blog and online magazine: *Inspired Ideas*. Amy lives in the Washington D.C. suburbs with her sweet husband, Rich, and their adorable son, Alfredo.

Amy's Clown Sundaes

Makes 1 clown sundae

- Your favorite ice cream, slightly softened for easy scooping
- Colorful cupcake wrappers, flattened
- Colored chocolate wafer melts
- Gel food coloring, your choice
- Ice cream cones
- Rainbow sprinkles
- Starburst candy, for mouth
- Maraschino cherries, for nose
- Chocolate chips/candy eyes {Wilton}
- Whipped cream

1. Scoop 1 ball of ice cream into flattened cupcake wrapper. Return to the freezer until ready to assemble.

2. Melt chocolate wafers melts in microwave {according to package instructions} in shallow pan, such as a pie dish. {If you are not able to find chocolate wafer melts in desired color, purchase white chocolate melts and add food coloring, 1 drop at a time.}

3. Working quickly, roll each ice cream cone in melted chocolate and shower with rainbow sprinkles. Set aside until chocolate hardens.

4. Cut slice from 1 Starburst candy, and work into mouth shape {1 candy makes 3 mouths}.

NOTE: If needed, warm candy in hands to make pliable.

5. Just before serving sundaes, remove from freezer and assemble: Place maraschino cherry nose in middle of ice cream ball; add chocolate chips or candy eyes, and mouth; top with sprinkle-coated hat; and add just a little bit of whipped cream on each side for hair.

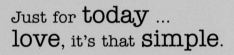

Just for today ...
love, it's that simple.

Festive
{Raking the Leaves}

Put on an extra sweater and get cozy with these sweet, festive autumn treats.

Ginger Molasses Cookies

Makes 24, depending on size

4	cups flour
4	tsp. baking soda {dissolved in small amount of hot water}
2½	tsp. cinnamon
1	tsp. cloves
1	tsp. ginger
¼	tsp. salt
1½	cups butter, softened
2	cups sugar, plus extra
2	eggs
½	cup molasses
24	candy corns

1. Preheat oven to 375ºF.

2. Mix together flour, baking soda mixture, cinnamon, cloves, ginger, and salt. Set aside.

3. In blender, beat butter and sugar until light and fluffy. Add eggs and molasses; beat well.

4. Slowly add dry ingredients to butter mixture until combined.

5. Roll dough into large balls, about 1½–2" {ice cream sandwiches require larger cookies}.

6. Fill bowl with extra sugar. Roll each ball in sugar until completely coated.

7. Place on cookie sheet with generous spacing. Bake 8–10 minutes.

8. Remove from oven, place 1 candy corn in each cookie, and cool.

ginger molasses
cookies

> Just for today ...
> be happy... everything
> does not have to be
> perfect to be happy.

Pumpkin Ice Cream Sandwich Cookies

Makes 6 to 8 servings

> 3 cups Pumpkin Pie Ice Cream, slightly softened {see recipe on page 20}
>
> Ginger Molasses Cookies {2 per sandwich}

1. Transfer Pumpkin Ice Cream into large, wide baking dish or pan so layer of ice cream will spread to approximately 1–1½" thick.

2. Smooth evenly and freeze. Once completely frozen, cut ice cream rounds a little smaller than Ginger Molasses Cookies. Remove from dish and smooth into perfect circle shapes. You can smooth it out once removed from dish.

3. Assemble sandwiches with ice cream in center of 2 cookies.

4. Eat immediately for a softer version, or refreeze sandwiches until completely firm.

Pumpkin Ice Cream Mini Tarts

Makes 12 mini tarts

12 mini Ginger Molasses Cookies
{see recipe on page 50}

3 cups Pumpkin Pie Ice Cream, softened
{see recipe on page 20}

1½ cups whipped cream, sweetened

Pecans, chopped; for garnish

Mini tart pan

Parchment paper

pumpkin
ice cream
mini
tarts

crunchy
pecans

sweetened
whipped
cream

pumpkin pie
ice cream

ginger
molasses
cookie
crust

1. Line each cup in mini tart pan with round piece of parchment paper to fit bottom {for easy removal}.

2. Place 1 mini Ginger Molasses Cookie on bottom of each tart cup; trim cookie to fit if needed.

3. Scoop Pumpkin Pie Ice Cream on top of each cookie, filling up tart cup; smooth out evenly.

4. Freeze at least 4 hours until firm, or overnight.

5. Once frozen, heat bottom of each tart cup with warm cloth; tart should pop out.

6. Garnish with whipped cream and pecans; serve immediately.

Apple Pecan Topping for Ice Cream

Makes 2 cups

- 6 fresh apples, peeled & sliced
- ½ cup brown sugar
- 1 tsp. cinnamon
- 2 tsp. butter, melted
- ¼–½ cup whole pecans {or any other nuts}
- Vanilla ice cream

1. Preheat oven to 350°F.

2. Spread fresh apples on cookie sheet.

3. Top with brown sugar, cinnamon, melted butter, and whole pecans; toss lightly.

4. Bake, stirring often until apples are soft and pecans are golden.

5. Remove from oven and serve over vanilla ice cream while still hot.

{ sprucing up the the vanilla }

Cozy Bowl Covers

All you need to make these cute bowl covers is an old sweater and some small bowls that will fit snuggly inside the sweater sleeves. 1 sweater will cover 4 bowls. Cut off the sweater sleeves {this is the only part of the sweater used}.

Place a bowl inside the sweater sleeve; measure the length needed to cover the bowl to its rim, making sure you have enough sleeve to wrap around the bottom of the bowl. Remove bowl, cut. Put the bowl back into the sleeve, and stitch the bottom closed. You may have to hem the top of the bowl too.

NOTE: For 2 of the bowls, you can use a sweater sleeve cuff as the top hem, which eliminates having to stitch a hem around the top of the cover. Covers can be easily removed to wash bowls.

keeping your **bowls** cozy

Just for today ...
look all around you
and feel content.

Candy Apples

Makes 8 apples

8	fresh apples, washed & dried
8	natural twigs/wooden sticks
1½	cups hot water
1	cup light corn syrup
2	cups sugar
½	cup red cinnamon candies/red food coloring
	Parchment paper
	Candy thermometer

1. Remove apple stems, and insert natural twigs or wooden sticks into apples.

2. Line baking sheet with parchment paper sprayed with nonstick cooking spray.

3. Combine hot water, light corn syrup, and sugar in saucepan over medium-high heat. Stir until sugar dissolves and mixture reaches 250°F.

4. Stir in red cinnamon candies or red food coloring to desired shade. Continue to cook until temperature reaches 285°F {hard-ball stage}.

5. Remove from heat and continue stirring until smooth. One by one, dip apples into mixture by tilting saucepan at an angle and rotating apples to cover completely. Place dipped apples on prepared baking sheet.

6. Let apples cool completely.

you are
"the | apple of my eye"

Meet My Friend Christine

Christine Hoffman is a designer, stylist, and pie baker. Her home and work have been featured in Where Women Cook and Country Living magazine, on HGTV and the DIY network, and in the role of event designer for The Creative Connection. Visit her blog at *www.piesandaprons.blogspot.ca*

Christine's Maple Walnut Ice Cream Pie

My pie tastes generally run to the classic fruit-filled or custard variety. I even like to stay purist by going without whipped cream or ice cream on my pie, so ice cream pies were generally not in my repertoire. This pie has changed my tune. Ice cream pies need not always be overly sweet, candy bar laden affairs or pastel kids' stuff. A combination of classic fall flavors and a rustic cornmeal crust make this an elegant ending to any autumn celebration.

Makes one 9-inch pie

CORNMEAL CARDAMOM BISCOTTI

- ½ cup butter, room temperature
- ¾ cup sugar
- 1 TB. pure maple syrup
- 1 tsp. vanilla extract
- 3 eggs
- 1¾ cups flour
- 1 cup yellow cornmeal
- 1 tsp. cardamom
- 1½ tsp. baking powder
- Parchment paper

PIE

- 15 Cornmeal Cardamom Biscotti {can use storebought}
- ½ cup butter
- ½ cup maple syrup
- 1 pint vanilla ice cream, softened
- 1 cup walnuts, toasted

CORNMEAL CARDAMOM BISCOTTI

1. Preheat oven to 350°F.
2. Cream butter and sugar together in medium bowl; stir in pure maple syrup and vanilla extract.
3. Add eggs and beat for 2 minutes until well-blended. Add remaining dry ingredients and stir until blended and smooth.
4. Divide dough into 4 equal parts onto 2 parchment-lined cookie sheets.
5. Pat each part into loaf shape, about ½" thick, 2" wide, and 12" long {dough will rise and spread during baking, so leave plenty of room!}.
6. Bake 20 minutes. Remove from oven, and let cool 15 minutes.
7. Slice loaves, and lay slices on unlined cookie sheets.
8. Bake an additional 15 minutes.
9. Let cool and cut into long pieces.

TO TOAST WALNUTS:

1. Preheat oven to 350°F.
2. Spread walnuts in single layer on small cookie sheet. Bake 10 minutes. Let cool.

PIE

1. Preheat oven to 325°F.
2. Place Cornmeal Cardamom Biscotti in food processor; process into fine crumbs. Add butter and pulse until blended. Using fingers, press crumb mixture into 9" glass pie pan to form crust.
3. Bake 15 minutes. Let cool completely.
4. In meantime, mix maple syrup into vanilla ice cream; place in freezer until firm, but not too hard.
5. Once crust is cool, fill with maple ice cream. Sprinkle with walnuts.
6. Freeze until set and ready to serve.

Christine's Rustic Pie Stand

To make a sweet and rustic pie stand, simply top a chunky wooden candlestick with a vintage metal pie or cake tin. Wrap a bit of sisal twine around the candlestick, and attach the pie plate to the candlestick with hot glue.

Festive
{Decking the Halls}

Brighten up the shortest and coldest days of the year with merry treats. Welcome the snow and get festive!

Cranberry Pistachio Ice Cream Chateaus

Makes 8, depending on mould size

ICE CREAM

- ½ cup pistachios, coarsely chopped
- 1 cup dried sweetened cranberries
- ½ cup almonds, slivered & toasted
- ¾ tsp. cinnamon
- 8 cups vanilla ice cream, softened
- 8¾ cup ice cream moulds/8 ramekins/4 glasses {water goblets to give ice cream a pear-shaped form}
- Parchment paper

TOPPING

- 7 oz. white chocolate
- ¼ cup almonds, slivered & toasted
- ¼ cup pistachios, chopped

1. Combine pistachios, dried sweetened cranberries, almonds, and cinnamon in bowl.

2. Add pistachio mixture to vanilla ice cream. Blend together until well-mixed.

3. Spoon mixture into ice cream moulds, ramekins, or glasses, making sure to smooth tops. Cover with plastic wrap. Freeze at least 5 hours or overnight until set.

4. Line baking tray with parchment paper. Remove ice cream from moulds by placing warm damp towel around moulds to soften ice cream and inverting moulds onto tray. Ice cream should just slide right out and onto tray. Pop back into freezer for at least 20 minutes to firm.

5. While ice cream is firming, make Topping. In double boiler over hot water, stir white chocolate until melted and smooth.

6. Remove hardened ice cream from freezer and place on individual serving plates. Top each one with melted chocolate and sprinkle with almonds and pistachios. Serve immediately.

Peppermint Bark

Makes 30 pieces

2	cups dark chocolate
10	cups white chocolate
10	peppermint candies, crushed
	Parchment paper

1. Melt dark chocolate and pour onto cookie sheet covered with parchment paper; spread evenly.

2. Place cookie sheet in refrigerator to firm.

3. Melt white chocolate, stirring in most of the peppermint candies.

4. Pour white chocolate mixture over hardened dark chocolate; spread evenly.

5. Add remaining candies on top.

6. Refrigerate until firm.

peppermint bark

not in keeping
but in giving

Festive Peppermint Ice Cream Pie

Makes one 9-inch pie

CRUST

- 4 hard peppermint candies
- 1 package chocolate wafer cookies
- 3 TB. sugar
- ½ cup butter, melted

FILLING

- 1 cup hard peppermint candies
- 5 cups vanilla ice cream, softened/or Candy Cane Ice Cream {see recipe on page 27}

GARNISH

- 2 hard peppermint candies, crushed

Note: If using Candy Cane Ice Cream, just pour into crust, as crushed candies are already in the homemade ice cream.

1. To make crust, place hard peppermint candies, chocolate wafer cookies, and sugar into blender or food processor. Process until very fine. Process butter into the mixture until well-combined.

2. Press mixture into 9" pie plate. Press evenly on bottom and sides of pan. Set aside.

3. To make filling, put peppermint candies into processor. Process until very fine. In large bowl, mix crushed candy with softened ice cream. Transfer into pie crust; smooth and add garnish.

4. Freeze at least 5 hours or overnight.

5. For easy cutting, let thaw a few minutes before serving.

Gratitude turns what we have into enough

melody beattie

festive peppermint pie

Mini Snowmen In a Glass

Chocolate sauce

Vanilla ice cream, softened

White nonpareils sprinkles for body

Orange vermicelli sprinkles for nose

Chocolate sugar ball sprinkles for eyes & mouth

Stick pretzels for arms

Small shot glasses/mini drinking glasses

1. Fill bottom of shot glasses or mini glasses with chocolate sauce, just enough to see it in bottom of glasses.

2. Carefully spoon vanilla ice cream on top of chocolate sauce until glass is filled just below rim. Put glasses of ice cream in freezer to harden while making heads.

3. Make round little balls for heads from vanilla ice cream. Place on cookie sheet and in freezer until firm, about 20 minutes.

4. Once heads are firm, place on top of filled ice cream glasses. Smooth around edges to form neck.

5. Sprinkle entire head and top of glass with white nonpareils sprinkles. Add 1 orange vermicelli sprinkle for nose, 2 sugar ball sprinkles for eyes and several for mouth, and 2 stick pretzels for arms.

6. Refreeze until firm.

Girlfriends

Make your own cirlce of snowwomen friends and decorate each with your favorite festive finds!

sprucing up the vanilla

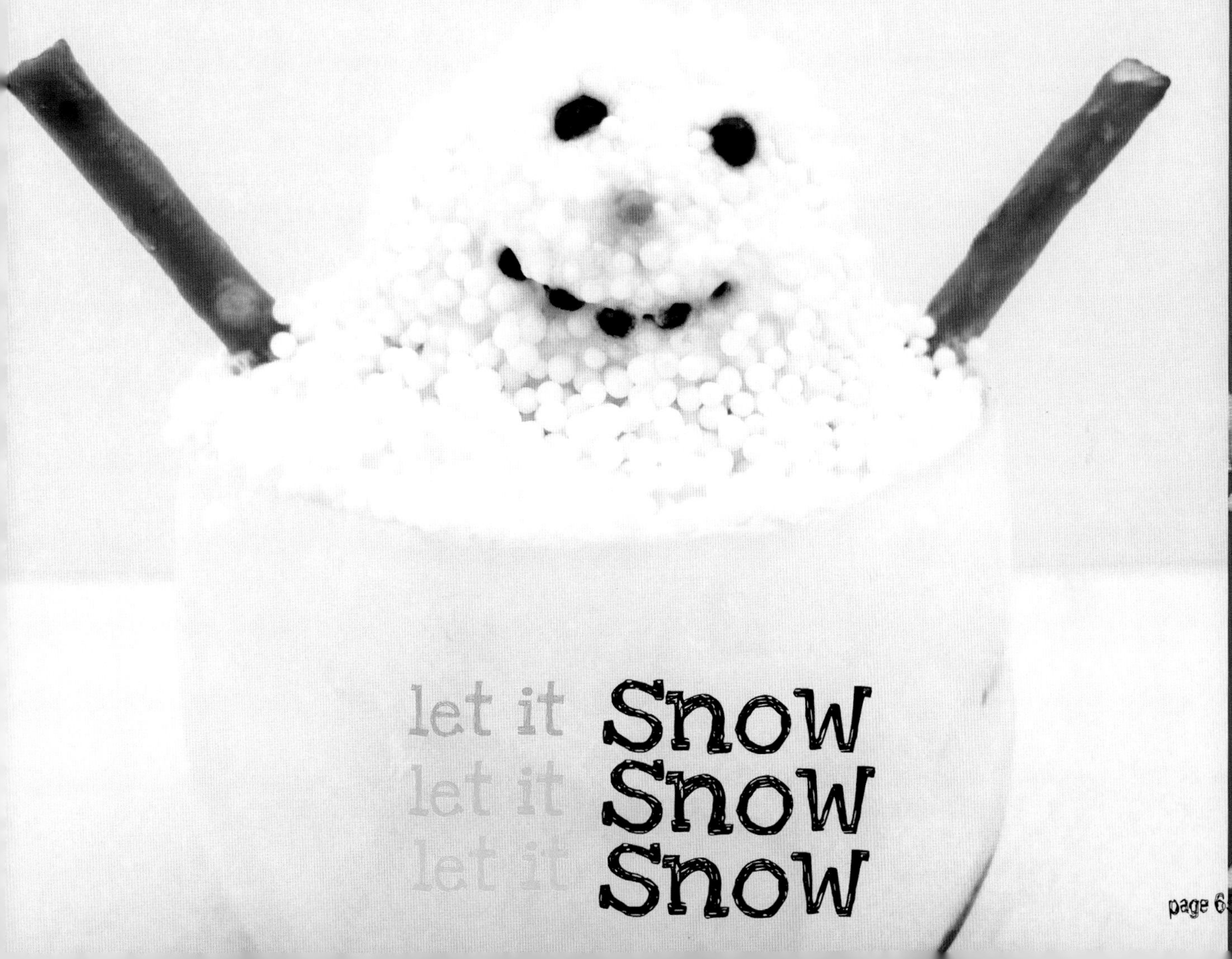

let it **Snow**
let it **Snow**
let it **Snow**

Meet My Friend Carol

My friend Carol told me the following story about her Silent Night Snowball Christmas tradition ... "I love Christmas and the traditions that come with it. Many years ago, while thinking of what to fix for dessert for our Christmas dinner, I came across a package of ice cream snowballs in the freezer section of the supermarket. There were exactly 6 — perfect for our family! For several years they always were right there, until 1 year ... no more snowballs! What to do now? Now that the tradition had begun, we could not go without. So, I began to make my own — vanilla ice cream shaped into balls, rolled in snowy coconut, a holly sprig {artificial, of course} for that festive touch ... and a candle to top it off!

Now, 30-something years later and with a family of 4 children, all married, and 12 grandkids, that's quite a few snowballs to make. They'll be made ahead, sometimes recruiting help, put into the freezer, and when the turkey and trimmings are all enjoyed on Christmas Day, it's snowball time. Each snowball is presented on a white paper doily, the candles are lit, lights are dimmed, and the procession begins with the singing of "Silent Night." There's a sparkle in the eyes of the children and adults alike as each receives their snowball. The tradition would not be the same without a little fun, so we play, who can keep their candle burning the longest? We know who started that tradition, but we're not telling!"

Just for today ...
count your
blessings.

Silent Night
Snowballs

Doily Apron

Embroidered pillowcase
Lace ribbon
Variety of dollies & lace

1. Cut pillowcase in half. Sew open end shut.

2. To make the tie, sew a long piece of lace ribbon to top half of pillow case, making sure ribbon is long enough to tie around and into a bow.

3. Cut doilies if necessary, and arrange doilies and other lace pieces on front with pins. Sew onto apron.

Meet My Friend Teresa

Teresa lives on an island in the Northwest and loves a fur ball named Doogan. She is the author of *Blooming on Bainbridge*, a blog where she writes about life on Bainbridge Island, favorite recipes, adventures in the Northwest, and learning to sew. Teresa is a Southern girl at heart. She loves sugar cookies and strawberry jam piled high on animal crackers. She enjoys practicing yoga and hiking trails with her husband Greg. Teresa created Bags by Bloom where she sells happy bags handmade with lots of JOY!

Teresa's Snow Ice Cream
Furry friends love Snow Ice Cream!

Makes 6 servings

	Big bowl of fresh clean snow
1	egg
1½	cups whole milk
	Vanilla sauce, to drizzle
1	cup sugar
	Sprinkles {optional}

1. Go outside and scoop up some fresh clean snow. Bring snow inside.

2. In separate bowl, whisk egg. Add whole milk; whisk until foamy with bubbles. Drizzle vanilla sauce. Continue to whisk. Add sugar and whisk.

3. Begin adding snow; whisk and stir. Soon it will be a big bowl of snow ice cream. Scoop ice cream into fancy cup and sprinkle to your heart's desire.

Marshmallow Snowmen on a Stick

Makes 8 snowmen

BODY

- 24 large white marshmallows
- 1 package {2 cups} vanilla wafer melts {white with sprinkles}

  Assorted sprinkles for eyes & nose

  Rocket candies for buttons

  Stick pretzels for arms
- 8 long kebob sticks

  Parchment paper

HATS

  Blue/any color vanilla wafer melts
- 8 large marshmallows, halved

1. Insert 1 kebob stick into 3 large white marshmallows. Repeat for all kebob sticks.

2. Melt vanilla wafer melts in tall microwaveable container that will cover all 3 marshmallows when dipped. Stir until smooth.

3. Assemble each snowman 1 at a time: Quickly dip each snowman into vanilla mixture and place on cookie sheet covered with parchment paper. Immediately add assorted sprinkles for eyes and nose, rocket candies for buttons, and pretzels for arms. Let cool until completely set.

4. Meanwhile, make hats by melting blue or any color vanilla wafer melts in microwavable bowl. Pour small amount of melted wafers onto piece of wax paper and, using a spatula, quickly spread into thin circle larger than the marshmallow. This will be the brim of the hat. Make 8 circles.

5. Dip each halved marshmallow into blue melted wafers and place directly on top of round circles. Let cool completely to set. Once set, hats should just peel off.

6. Place each hat on top of snowman using a little bit of melted blue wafers as glue.

marshmallow
Snowmen
it's a marshmallow world.....

Just for today ...
delight in small pleasures.

Rich

{having a full-bodied flavour filled with yummy goodness}

A little bite of these treats is all you need to make your taste buds happy, but rest assured, you will want to finish every last decadent morsel.

"Cup of Joe"
ice cream cake

a cup of joe...
*the American name
for a cup
of coffee*

"Cup of Joe"
Ice Cream Cake

Makes one 9-inch round cake

- 2½ TB. sugar
- ⅓ cup strong coffee, freshly brewed {espresso for stronger flavour}
- 4½ TB. coffee-flavoured liqueur {optional}
- 1 {9-inch} Vanilla Sponge Cake
- 4 TB. instant coffee crystals, sifted/crushed
- 8 cups Coffee Ice Cream {see recipe on page 23}
-   Very thin chocolate pieces {see recipe on page 81}
- 1 {9-inch} round spring-form pan

1. Stir sugar into freshly brewed strong coffee until dissolved. Add coffee-flavoured liqueur, and let syrup mixture cool.

2. Cut cooled Vanilla Sponge Cake in half horizontally, making 2 layers. Place 1 layer in bottom of 9" round spring-form pan. If necessary, trim cake to fit.

3. Brush half of syrup mixture on top of cake layer, and sprinkle top with half of instant coffee crystals.

4. Mix half of Coffee Ice Cream until soft and spreadable. Spread over top of cake.

5. Top with second cake layer {trim if needed} and brush with remaining syrup. Pop in freezer to firm up, about 30 minutes.

6. Sprinkle remaining 2 tablespoons coffee crystals over top of cake. Mix remaining 4 cups ice cream until softened, and spread over cake. Freeze until firm, about 5–6 hours or overnight.

7. Remove from spring-form pan and garnish with thin chocolate pieces before serving.

Vanilla Sponge Cake

Makes one 9-inch round cake

    ½ cup flour, plus extra for dusting

    ½ cup cornstarch

    4 eggs, separated

    ¾ cup sugar

    2 tsp. vanilla extract

    Pinch of salt

    Parchment paper

    Butter parchment

1. Preheat oven to 350°F. Line bottom of 9" round baking pan with parchment paper and butter parchment. Dust with flour and tap off excess.

2. Sift ½ cup flour and cornstarch together in small bowl; set aside.

3. Mix together egg yolks, ½ cup sugar, and vanilla extract with electric mixer. Beat on high for 3 minutes until mixture becomes pale in color.

4. Mix egg whites and salt in separate bowl for approximately 3 minutes, until soft peaks form. Mix in remaining ¼ cup sugar, a little bit at a time. Continue beating until stiff glossy peaks form, about 2–3 minutes.

5. Fold egg white mixture into yolk mixture. Gently fold in flour mixture, little bits at a time, until completely incorporated. Do not over-stir.

6. Pour mixture into pan and smooth top. Bake about 25 minutes or until cake tester comes out clean. Let cool on wire rack in pan. Once cool, remove from cake pans.

Just for today …
be enthusiastic about the success of others just as you are about your own.

Ribbon Cuffs

Turn brooches and ribbons into sweet cuffs.

You'll need old or new brooches and 1½–2-inch, pretty velvet or double satin ribbon. Use heavier weight ribbon so that it will hold the weight of the brooch.

Measure ribbon around your wrist, making sure to leave enough to tie before cutting.

Pin brooch onto ribbon and tie onto your wrist {or ask someone to help you}.

Mint Ice Cream Minis

Makes six 2-inch tarts

- 2 cups chocolate chip mint ice cream
- 6 Chocolate Wafer Crust moulds
  Hot Fudge Sauce {see recipe on page 157}
  Mint chocolate bar shavings

1. Place chocolate chip mint ice cream in bowl, and stir to soften.

2. Add enough ice cream over Chocolate Wafer Crust to fill moulds. Drizzle and swirl Hot Fudge Sauce onto top of ice cream to make a pretty pattern.

3. Transfer rings to freezer and let set for at least 4–5 hours or overnight.

4. To unmould, warm each ring with warm, wet dishcloth, and then shake gently until tart slides out. Garnish with mint chocolate bar shavings. Serve immediately.

Chocolate Wafer Crust

Makes si, 2-inch tarts

- 30 chocolate wafers
- 3 TB. sugar
- 4 TB. butter, melted
- 6 {2-inch} ring moulds

1. Preheat oven to 350°F.

2. Using food processor, blend chocolate wafers into fine crumbs. Add sugar and butter; process until well-combined.

3. Add 2 tablespoons of chocolate wafer mixture to bottom of each mould. Press firmly into bottom of moulds and halfway up sides.

4. Bake about 6–7 minutes. Transfer to wire rack and let cool completely before filling with chocolate mint ice cream.

mom's marshmallow rich fudge

Mom's Rich Marshmallow Fudge

Makes 24 pieces

- ¾ cup butter, plus extra to grease pan
- 4 cups sugar
- 1²⁄₃ cups evaporated milk
- 2 {6 oz.} packages semisweet chocolate chips
- 2 cups mini marshmallows
- 2 tsp. vanilla extract
- Candy thermometer

1. Butter 12" x 7" pan.

2. Combine butter, sugar, and evaporated milk in large saucepan over medium heat. Cook, stirring often until candy reaches soft-ball stage {until 235°F is reached on candy thermometer}.

3. Remove from heat and stir in semisweet chocolate chips, mini marshmallows, and vanilla extract.

4. Stir until completely melted. Pour into pan and let cool in refrigerator.

5. Once cool, slice and store in airtight container in refrigerator.

{love you mom}

ribbon joy
pile it on

Ribbon Tins

These decorative tins make great gift containers to give your Mom's Rich Marshmallow Fudge to firends, or they make usefull, yet pretty, pen and pencil holders. Clean and remove labels from soup cans or canned vegetable tins. Cut assorted ribbons to fit around tins. Tie evenly around tins, and fill with goodies for giving.

Ribbon Hanger

Hang above your work desk or sewing space to add some fun into your life. Prefect for a babies room to hang above the crib or a little girls room to add a special decorative touch.

Cut assorted ribbons into 18–20" lengths; leave extra to tie. Tie ribbons onto large embroidery hoop {8" or larger, depending on desired hanger size}. Once tied on, cut ribbons at various lengths so the bottom is uneven.

Cream Cookie Pie

Makes one 9-inch pie

- 1 {11 oz.} package vanilla cream chocolate cookies {enough to line a pie dish}
- 3 cups vanilla ice cream
- 2 cups Tempered Thin Chocolate Pieces
- 2 cups chocolate ice cream, plus extra to scoop on top of pie {optional}
- 2 cups whipping cream

  Sugar, to taste

  Vanilla extract, to taste

1. Line 9" pie pan or plate with vanilla cream chocolate cookies, including sides. Put in freezer to set for 20 minutes.

2. Put vanilla ice cream into bowl; stir to soften. Scoop over top of cookie layer, and smooth with spatula.

3. Add a layer of Tempered Thin Chocolate Pieces {reserving some for garnish on top of pie}. Freeze 2–3 hours until firm.

4. Stir chocolate ice cream to soften, and ice cream layer on top of chocolate pieces. Freeze 4–5 hours or overnight, until very firm.

5. Remove pie from freezer, and let sit while whipping cream {add sugar and vanilla extract to taste}. Spread whipped cream on top of pie just before serving; garnish with reserved thin chocolate pieces.

OPTIONAL: Add scoops of chocolate ice cream to top before serving.

cream cookie

ice cream pie

Tempered Thin Chocolate Pieces

Makes 2 cups

    1 {3.5 oz.} good quality dark chocolate bar
    Parchment paper

1. Cover cookie sheet with parchment paper.

2. Break dark chocolate bar into small pieces for fast melting.

3. Using double boiler, bring about 3" of water to boil Once boiling, turn water down to a simmer so that chocolate does not reach a temperature over 90ºF.

4. Add chocolate pieces to upper pan of double boiler, and place on top of simmering water. Let chocolate melt slowly while stirring constantly. Be patient, and keep temperature on low or chocolate will end up being clumpy and will not set properly.

5. Stir until most of chocolate is melted and remove from heat; continue to stir until smooth.

NOTE: Make sure to wipe bottom of pan to remove water drips; do not let water enter the chocolate mixture. Just one drop of water will spoil the chocolate mixture. Water and chocolate do not mix!

6. Pour chocolate onto centre of prepared cookie sheet. Spread into thin layer with spatula.

7. Let chocolate set in fridge for at least 1 hour. Remove and break into nice thin pieces.

Just for today ...
play tag with your joy ...
pass some on to all you meet.

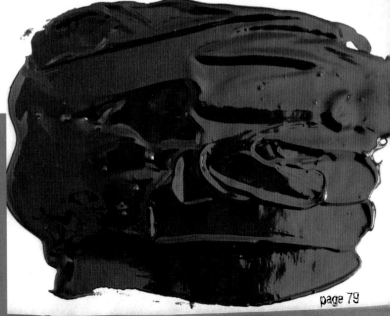

Cherries Dipped in Chocolate & Pistachios

Makes 24 large cherries

       Fresh cherries, stems on, cleaned

  1 {10 oz.} package chocolate chips, melted

  ¾ cup pistachios, crushed

1. Dip fresh cherries into melted chocolate chips and then immediately into pistachios.

2. Place on wax paper to dry.

dip
dunk
douse
drench

Hot Chocolate Ice Cream Cubes

Makes 1 ice cube tray

Simple Vanilla Bean Ice Cream
(see recipe on page 10)

Ice cube tray

Little spoons/Popsicle sticks

Hot chocolate, ready to serve

1. Soften Simple Vanilla Bean Ice Cream just a bit, and add to ice cube trays; smooth top. Immediately insert little spoons or Popsicle sticks, and pop into freezer.

2. Freeze solid for no less than 5 hours — easier to pop out of trays if frozen solid.

3. Heat bottom of each cube section with warm dishtowel. Tug gently on the stick or spoon; the ice cream cube should just easily pop out.

4. Pop immediately into cup of steaming hot chocolate. Stir and enjoy.

sprucing up
the
vanilla

melt . . . stir . . . sip . . . .
. . . stir . . . sip . . . melt
melt . . . . stir

Rich Hot Cocoa Mix

Makes 3½ cups

    2 cups dry powered milk
    1 cup sifting sugar
    ½ cup cocoa
    ⅓ cup powdered non-dairy creamer

1. Mix all ingredients together with whisk.

2. Store in airtight container until packaging to give away.

hot cocoa never looked so sweet

Just for today ... remember life is here and now so don't miss it.

Hot Cocoa Giveaway Jars

Each jar has enough cocoa for 1 serving. These are perfect for gift giving.

I used mini jam jars, but any small jar will work as long as it holds 4 tablespoons of cocoa mix with enough room left over to add marshmallows.

Make Rich Hot Cocoa Mix and scoop 4 tablespoons into a mini jar. Fill rest of jar with mini marshmallows. Be careful not to shake too much. Top lid with a sweet cupcake liner tied with a string or ribbon.

Meet My Friend Maaike

Maaike van Koert grew up baking and crafting in the Netherlands. After moving to Canada with her newly wedded husband in 2011, she decided to set aside her management consulting career and spend her days doing what she loves most: crafts, photography, design, and baking. On her light and fresh blog, *crejjtion.blogspot.com*, she keeps track of her creative adventures and shares the results with the rest of the world.

Maaike's Chocolate Cherry Cream Parfait

Serves 8

- 1 {18 oz.} can cherries
- 1 tsp. cinnamon
- ¼ cup unsalted butter
- 1¼ cups dark semisweet chocolate chips
- 3 eggs, seperated
- 1 cup icing sugar
- 3 cups whipping cream

Just for **today** ...
remember worrying **never** solves **anything**.

1. Wrap rectangular 7" baking tin in plastic wrap to prevent parfait from sticking to mould.

2. Empty can of cherries, including juice, into bowl; add cinnamon.

3. Melt unsalted butter and semisweet chocolate chips together in microwave until nicely mixed, thick, and shiny. Be careful not to burn it: Microwave 10 seconds or less at a time and stir in between; set aside

4. Mix egg yolks with ½ cup icing sugar until fluffy; set aside. In separate bowl, beat egg whites until stiff.

5. In another bowl, beat whipping cream until stiff.

6. For the cherry layer, mix ⅓ of whipped cream with ¼ cup sugar. With a tablespoon, add cherry juice to whipped cream until it becomes softly pink, about 5–6 tablespoons should do. Add half of cherry mixture and stir through whipped cream. Put mixture in prepared baking tin. Put a few more cherries on top of this layer to taste.

7. For the creamy layer, add ¼ cup sugar and mix into half remaining whipped cream.

8. Put creamy layer on top of cherry layer until fully covered.

9. For the chocolate layer, mix chocolate/butter mixture with egg yolks/sugar mixture. Add all remaining whipped cream and beat egg whites to mix.

NOTE: It is not a problem when chocolate does not blend in evenly; it will create little bites in the parfait that are delicious.

10. Add chocolate layer on top of creamy layer.

11. Put parfait in freezer for at least 3–5 hours. Don't stir. Take out 10 minutes before serving and cut into slices.

Maaike's Cupcake Garland

Cotton twine

Needle

Little colored cupcake liners

1. Cut twine approximately 60" long.

2. Tie a simple knot about 10" from the end to make sure there is enough thread left to make a loop to hang it somewhere.

3. With needle on longest side of thread, go through one cupcake liner from bottom up.

4. Take another liner and, with needle, go through it the other way around, from the inside out.

5. Make liners go down the twine until they reach the knot, and then make another knot right behind second liner.

6. Leave about 2", and tie knot.

7. Repeat, adding on liners until there is 10" left over, enough to make a loop to hang this end as well.

NOTE: You can vary the garland by adding different sizes and colors of cupcake liners.

Meet My Friend Kari

Kari Friesen believes that there's no sweeter gift than one from the heart!

Kari is a stay-at-home mom who loves to create little treasures for those around her. With a toddler and a new baby on the way, she finds there's no shortage of projects!

Kari's Black Forest Ice Cream Cake

Serves 12

- 2 8" round Kari's Rich Chocolate Cakes
- 4 cups vanilla ice cream, softened
- 1 cup fresh cherries, pitted & sliced
- 2 {18 oz.} cans cherry pie filling

GARNISH

- 2 cups whipped cream, sweetened
- Chocolate shavings
- Whole fresh cherries for garnish

1. Freeze 2 Kari's Rich Chocolate Cakes until ready to assemble.
2. Mix vanilla ice cream with fresh cherries.
3. Assemble cake in 1, 8" spring-form pan to keep it all together while freezing solid.

TO ASSEMBLE CAKE:

1. Start with 1 cake {it should just fit inside the spring-form pan; if it's too big, cut around edges to fit}, add half of the ice cream mixture, spreading evenly on top.
2. Follow with half of cherry pie filling to cover ice cream mixture. Top with the last 8" cake round.
3. Pop completed cake back into freezer for at least 6–8 hours, or overnight.
4. Once cake is completely frozen, remove from spring-form pan. Top with whipped cream, chocolate shavings, and handful of fresh cherries.
5. Serve immediately. Can be refrozen if not completely eaten.

cheery **cherries**

Kari's Rich Chocolate Cake

Makes two 8-inch cakes

- ¾ cup cocoa, plus extra for dusting
- 2 cups flour
- 2 cups sugar
- 1½ tsp. baking soda
- 1½ tsp. baking powder
- ¼ tsp. salt
- 2 eggs
- 1 cup whole milk
- ½ cup vegetable oil
- 2 tsp. vanilla extract
- 1 cup water, boiling

1. Preheat oven to 350°F. Grease and dust 2, 8" layer cake pans with cocoa.

2. In large bowl, sift together cocoa, flour, sugar, baking soda, baking powder, and salt. With electric mixer, blend in eggs, whole milk, vegetable oil, and vanilla extract until well-combined. Slowly add boiling water into cake batter. Mix well; batter will be runny.

3. Pour batter into 2 prepared pans. Bake 30–35 minutes. When done, tops should feel firm and cake tester will come out clean. Cool 5 minutes, remove from pans, and cool completely on wire racks.

Kari's Black Forest Cake in a Jar

Serves 12

1. Kari's Rich Chocolate Cake {see recipe on page 87}

2. {18 oz.} cans cherry pie filling

3. cups whipped cream, sweetened with vanilla & sugar to taste

1. large dark chocolate bar, coarsely grated

1. {1-gal.} jar

are you an Apron girl?

1. Break up 1 completely cooled Kari's Rich Chocolate Cake into bite-sized pieces.

2. Add layer of cake to bottom of jar, followed by 1 layer cherry pie filling and 1 layer whipped cream. Continue this pattern until many layers are formed, ending with whipped cream and dark chocolate pieces.

3. Refrigerate until ready to serve. Use long-handled serving spoon to dish out.

Kari's Cake Bunting

Pretty cardstock {2-sided}
Coordinating embroidery cotton
Large pointed needle

1. Cut cardstock into little triangles, depending on desired size.

2. Cut embroidery cotton to desired length for bunting.

3. Thread large pointed needle with coordinating embroidery cotton and sew several stitches through top of each triangle, leaving even spaces between triangles. Pull thread all the way through; repeat.

Ripe

{heavenly indulgences that contain the sweetness of freshly picked fruits}

Celebrate with the fresh flavours of summer all year long; light, refreshing and so satisfying these treats are a joy to eat because they seem almost guilt free.

Raspberry Red Sorbet

Makes 6 cups

- 3 cups water
- ¾ cup sugar
- 6 cups fresh/frozen raspberries, plus extra fresh raspberries for topping
- ¼ cup raspberry jam

1. Combine water and sugar in saucepan. Bring to boil; simmer until sugar has dissolved. Add fresh or frozen raspberries.

2. Once mixture has cooled, purée in food processor or blender. Add raspberry jam and blend until mixed.

3. Pour mixture through sieve into large bowl to remove all seeds.

4. Pour seedless mixture into 2 metal baking pans for freezing; in this case, metal is better for faster freezing. Place flat in freezer.

5. Make sure to stir mixture every 30 minutes, scraping the frozen sides and mixing frozen pieces into unfrozen center.

6. After about 4 hours, add frozen mixture back into blender to purée bigger chunks so consistency is finer. Be careful not to allow mixture to melt too much.

7. Scoop into individual bowls and top with fresh raspberries. Serve immediately.

NOTE: This recipe can be made with any other berries.

Summer brights that are deliciously refreshing

Easy Melon Sorbet

Makes 6 cups

Fast, easy, and oh so refreshing! My favorite is watermelon, but cantaloupe and honeydew are just as yummy. An easy summer dessert you can make in minutes; just have the melon sliced and frozen, waiting to be blended.

Cut up a cantaloupe, honeydew, or small seedless watermelon into cubes. Freeze until solid; freezer bags work well for storing cubed melons in the freezer. Once melon cubes are frozen, put into a food processor or blender and purée. To smooth, add a little water. Sweeten to taste. Sorbet is now ready to serve or can be stored in freezer until ready eat.

watermelon

cantaloupe

Strawberry Sorbet

Makes 6 cups

> 3⅓ cups fresh ripe strawberries
>
> Juice from 1 fresh orange
>
> Juice from 1 fresh lemon
>
> 1 cup sugar

1. Purée fresh ripe strawberries with fresh orange and fresh lemon juice in blender or food processor. Stir in sugar, and let mixture sit 1-2 hours; stir often until all sugar has dissolved completely.

2. Pour mixture into ice cream maker's freezer cylinder and follow manufacturer's directions until thick and smooth.

OR

1. Freeze mixture in shallow container until frozen but not firm.

2. Pour into mixing bowl and beat until mixture is broken up and smooth.

3. Return to freezer until firm and ready to serve.

Strawberry
hearts
to you

sorbet
Strawberry

loving spoonfuls

Beaded Spoons

These little spoons are perfect for adding a little pizazz to a simple dessert. They take no time to make; all that is needed are some small spoons with smooth handles, pliable wire, pliers, and large seed beads {make sure beads are color-washable; dye will come off of some beads, leaving you with all clear beads}.

This idea was borrowed from a spoon I received many years ago as a gift; this spoon still looks as good as new and is used often.

Starting at base of the spoon, wrap wire around the handle, making sure to leave a bit on the end to make a fancy scroll design; this is where the pliers come in handy.

Wrap wire tightly and add the beads as you go up the spoon's handle. Finish off with another scroll to keep the beads and wire secure.

Pretty Embellishments ...
Adding a Button or Two

It is so easy to take an ordinary dress, sweater, or blouse and turn it into something extraordinary just by adding a few fancy buttons or brooches. Wherever I go, I am always looking for pretty buttons. By just adding or changing the buttons on a piece of clothing, you can change its entire look — a perfect and inexpensive way to freshen up your wardrobe.

add some *Sparkle* to your life

Just for today ... be the **sparkling** jewel that **lights** up the **world**.

Strawberry Curd

This curd is very versatile and can be used like a lemon curd to spread over scones, toast, and ice cream, or as a cake or tart filling.

Strawberry Curd is the perfect gift to give when put into little decorative jars.

Makes 3 cups

- 3 cups fresh strawberries, sliced
- 3 tsp. cornstarch
- ½ cup sugar
- * Zest of 1 fresh lime
- *¼ cup fresh lime juice
- 3 small eggs yolks
- 1½ tsp. vanilla extract
- ½ tsp. salt

  *Fresh lemon zest and fresh lemon juice can be substituted

1. Cook strawberries in saucepan over medium-low heat. Stir often until cooked and runny, about 10 or more minutes, crushing up berries while stirring. Set aside.

2. In bowl, combine cornstarch, salt, sugar, and zest of 1 fresh lime. Stir in fresh lime juice until well-blended.

3. Whisk egg yolks with vanilla extract and slowly drizzle into cornstarch mixture, whisking constantly.

4. Slowly whisk cornstarch mixture into hot strawberry mixture; whisk until well-blended.

5. Place mixture over medium-low heat and bring to boil, stirring constantly until mixture thickens. Set aside to cool.

6. Once cooled, put in small gift jars or store in refrigerator until ready to use or to give-away. Refrigerated curd should keep for several months.

Strawberry Curd {made with a handful of bliss}

Strawberry Cream Tarts

Makes 6 tarts

- 1 cup whipping cream
- ¼ cup sugar
- 1 tsp. vanilla extract
- ¾ cups Strawberry Curd {see recipe on page 97}
- Fresh strawberries/Dried Strawberry Decorations
- Tart Shells in Jars/premade store-bought frozen pie dough in jars

1. Whip whipping cream with sugar and vanilla extract; stir in Strawberry Curd until well-mixed.

2. Fill Tart Shells in Jars or premade store-bought frozen pie dough in jars with whipped curd mixture. Refrigerate until ready to serve.

3. Top with fresh strawberries or Dried Strawberries Decorations just before serving.

Tart Shells in Jars

{My Mom's Pie Crust}

- 2½ cups flour
- ½ lb. lard {Tenderflake}, cubed
- ½ cup cold water
- 6 very small canning jars {size may vary}

CAUTION: this cooking method is not recommended by the manufacturers of canning jars; it is used at your own risk due to the possibility of jars breaking while being baked.

1. Preheat oven to 350ºF.

2. Add 2 cups flour to lard and mix by hand or with pastry blender until well-combined. Add cold water; mix well.

3. Hand knead remaining ½ cup flour into dough on lightly floured board until you can roll dough into soft ball. If dough is sticky, add a little more flour.

4. Roll dough out, and cut to fit each jar; 2 rectangle pieces per jar works well. Fold dough over edges of jar. Prick bottoms with fork.

5. Bake approximately 10 minutes or until golden brown; checking to make sure crust is not burning or jars have not cracked.

6. Let cool completely before filling.

Dried Strawberry Decorations

I like to dry strawberry slices for decorating or to put in my homemade granola. If you don't have a food dehydrator, the oven works just as well.

Cut strawberries into thin slices of even thicknesses. Place berries in a dehydrator or on baking sheets lined with parchment paper to dry in the oven, spreading out berries in a single layer. Turn on oven to its lowest setting, and place baking trays in oven for a 10–12 hour period; make sure you turn berries once or twice during this time period.

Cool berries completely before storing in an airtight container in a cool, dark place. If berries are not completely dry, they could rot; extra time may be needed to dry in the oven or dried berries can be left out on the counter for a day.

strawberry curd + whipped cream = more please

Strawberry Pincushions

I have always adored these sweet vintage-like pincushions and just knew I had to include them with the strawberry recipes. Growing up, my grandma had some of these in her sewing box, so every time I see them sweet memories come flooding back.

Tissue or paper for pattern

Little bits of fabric

Needle & matching thread

Green embroidery floss

Small jar/container

Rice/fine sand for filling strawberries

Green felt pieces for strawberry caps

Fabric glue

1. Trace a circle onto paper double the size you want the strawberry to be; cut out. Fold circle in half.

2. Trace pattern onto fabric piece and cut out.

3. Shape fabric into cone shape with right sides together; hand stitch up side with matching thread, making a side seam. Turn so that right side of fabric is facing out.

4. Sew a running stitch along top of cone; this will easily gather top to close.

5. Stand cone upright on top of small jar or container for easy filling. Fill with rice or fine sand. Pull running stich tight, and stitch top closed.

6. Cut small felt cap for strawberry. Sew on loop handle to cap top made from six pieces of embroidery floss; knot inside. Glue felt cap onto top of strawberry.

it's a berry lovely pincushion

Rhubarb Strawberry Crisp

This old-fashioned dessert takes just minutes to prepare. Crisps can be made with any fruit, but this is one of my favorite flavour combinations — the rhubarb's tartness mixed with the sweet berries and served with a scoop of vanilla ice cream is pure joy.

Makes one 9x13-inch pan

FRUIT MIXTURE

- 4 cups fresh strawberries, sliced
- 4 cups rhubarb, sliced
- ¾ cups sugar
- 1 TB. flour
- 1 tsp. cinnamon

TOPPING

- ¾ cup butter, cubed
- 1 cup flour
- 1 cup rolled oats
- 1 cup brown sugar
- 1½ tsp. cinnamon

1. Preheat oven to 375ºF.

2. Combine fresh strawberries and rhubarb with sugar, flour, and cinnamon. Pour into greased 13" x 9" baking pan.

3. Make topping by combining butter, flour, rolled oats, brown sugar, and cinnamon with a pastry blender until well-blended. Spread over top of fruit mixture.

4. Bake at 375ºF for 40–45 minutes, until fruit is bubbly and topping is golden brown.

rhubarb-strawberry Crisp

Fresh Cherry Chocolate Chunk Ice Cream

In our home, we like to take vanilla ice cream and spruce it up a bit by adding our favorite taste combinations. My husband's favorite dessert is Black Forest Cake because he loves the flavours of rich chocolate and cherries together. So every so often I will "spruce up his vanilla" with these favorite flavours.

Start with a big bowl of softened vanilla ice cream. Add fresh sliced cherry pieces {we love juicy dark Bing cherries} and dark chocolate chunks from a very good-quality chocolate bar; mix together by hand. You control how much you want to add of each. Spoon into serving dishes and don't forget the fresh cherry on top!

Sprucing up
the vanilla

Pineapple Cream

This delicious shake-like drink has no ice cream but lots of fresh whipped cream. If you like pineapple, this is one treat you will want to try.

Top your drink with a pretty dried pineapple flower, relax in your favorite chair, and start dreaming of Hawaii.

    2 {14 oz.} cans crushed pineapple
    2 TB. fresh lemon juice
    2 TB. fresh lime juice
   ¼ cup sugar, plus 1 tsp.
    1 cup whipping cream
    1 tsp. vanilla extract

1. Drain pineapple, and reserve 3 tablespoons of juice.

2. In large bowl, blend together pineapple, fesh lemon and fresh lime juice, ¼ cup sugar, and pineapple juice. Freeze 1–2 hours, until slushy.

3. Whip whipping cream with 1 teaspoon sugar and vanilla extract. Stir whipped cream into slushy pineapple.

4. Pour into individual glasses and freeze 1 hour before serving with a spoon.

Pineapple Flowers

These flowers are made from oven-dried pineapple slices. They are delicious to eat and make a sweet embellishment on any dessert.

Preheat oven to 225ºF. Peel pineapple and slice very thin. The thinner the slices, the brighter yellow the flowers will be. Once sliced, cut little triangles around the edges; these will be the petal edges and will remove any little brown bits known as "eyes."

Place pineapple slices on a baking sheet lined with parchment paper. Make sure slices are not overlapping; two baking sheets may be needed.

Let bake until tops look dried, about 30 minutes. Turn slices, and continue to dry for about another 30 minutes. Cool on wire rack. Slices will keep up to 3–4 days in an airtight container; keep refrigerated.

and Blueberry

Lemon Blueberry Ice Cream Pie

The tart lemony flavour comes through loud and clear in this delicious pie made with fresh lemon curd. The blueberries add a beautiful color to this pretty pie.

Try this pie with Strawberry Curd as well {see recipe on page 97 substituting blueberries for strawberries.}

Makes one 9-inch pie

SHORTBREAD PIE CRUST

    1½ cups shortbread cookie crumbs, finely crushed
    2 TB. sugar
    5 TB. butter, melted

1. Preheat oven to 375°F.

2. Mix shortbread cookie crumbs, sugar, and butter together until well-blended.

3. Press mixture into the bottom of a 9" pie plate.

4. Bake 8–10 minutes. Let cool on rack.

NOTE: I used shortbread cookie crumbs, but you can use graham cracker, gingersnap, or vanilla wafer crumbs.

LEMON CURD

    2 cups sugar
    ½ cup butter, cubed
    3 TB. fresh lemon zest
      Juice from 7 medium fresh lemons, just over 1 cup
    4 large eggs

1. Add sugar, butter, fresh lemon zest, and fresh lemon juice into large saucepan and cook over medium heat until sugar and butter melt.

2. Beat large eggs in medium-sized bowl and slowly add ½ cup hot lemon mixture into egg mixture; mix well while adding.

look for *the beauty* of this *Day*

3. Add egg mixture back into rest of hot lemon mixture and continue to cook over low heat until mixture thickens {about 12 minutes}, stirring constantly.

4. Once mixture is thick, remove from heat and let cool completely; curd will keep up to 2 weeks in refrigerator if kept in airtight container.

ASSEMBLING LEMON BLUEBERRY ICE CREAM PIE

        4 cups vanilla ice cream
        1 Shortbread Pie Crust
    1½ cups Lemon Curd
        1 cup fresh/frozen blueberries
            Meringue Topping

1. Add 2 cups vanilla ice cream over Shortbread Pie Crust; spread evenly.

2. Top ice cream with ¾ cup Lemon Curd and swirl gently, slightly mixing into ice cream.

3. Sprinkle ½ cup fresh or frozen blueberries on top.

4. Repeat layers, ending with blueberries.

5. Freeze pie until solid, at least 4 hours or overnight before adding Meringue Topping.

6. Spread Meringue Topping over pie. Put pie under broiler until meringue turns golden brown; watch constantly this should take only seconds {less than 50 seconds}.

7. Put pie back into the freezer to firm before serving.

MERINGUE TOPPING

        2 egg whites
    1¼ cups sugar
        1 TB. light corn syrup
    1½ tsp. vanilla extract

1. Preheat oven to broil with rack approximately 8-9" from heat.

2. In blender, mix together all ingredients until soft peaks form; blend for 10 or more minutes.

Meet My Friend Cathie

Cathie Avraam loves to bake, make, and create. She has two little beings in her life and they are her inspiration to create things. Cathie loves to inspire them as well, and together they make lasting memories.

Cathie blogs about her recipes, photographs, and bits of her family's life, hoping to inspire others to bake something they never thought they could or create a keepsake with their children. You can visit Cathie's blog, *melbourneepicure.blogspot.com*.

Cathie's Blackberry Swirl Semifreddo

Makes 8 cups

- 3 cups fresh blackberries/2 cups frozen blackberries
- 3 TB. icing sugar
- 3 eggs
- 2 egg yolks
- 1 tsp. vanilla extract
- 1 cup sugar
- 2 cups cream

1. Process fresh blackberries and 1 tablespoon icing sugar in food processor until smooth; set aside. If using frozen berries, place in small saucepan over low heat, heat for a few minutes, add 1 tablespoon icing sugar, and stir to dissolve. Using food processor, blend until smooth; return to low heat for another few minutes. Set aside to cool

2. Place eggs and egg yolks, vanilla extract, and 1 cup sugar in heatproof bowl over a saucepan of simmering water; whisk mixture with hand-held beater for about 8 minutes or until heated, thick, and pale — it will look like custard. Remove from heat, and beat for another 8 minutes until cool.

3. Whisk cream until stiff peaks form, and then gently fold egg mixture into the cream until just combined.

4. Pour into 8-cup capacity pan, and spoon over fruit mixture.

5. Using a knife, swirl mixture through cream.

6. Freeze for about 6 hours or until firm.

Cathie's Fabric Picture Cards

Gather together fabric scraps. Place a piece of baking paper under your work area to prevent the fusible webbing from sticking to your ironing board, and then iron paper-backed fusible webbing to the back of different fabric scraps, following manufacturer's instructions.

Cut out shapes for the picture, peel the paper from the webbing, and arrange the shapes onto your card. Iron using medium heat without steam.

Don't forget to create other themed cards.

Meet My Friend Trisha

Trisha Brink attended the Art Institute of Seattle for residential interior design. When she isn't whipping up ice cream for her hubby and two young sons, she uses her gifts and talents working with others in the retail design community as a stylist, designer, buyer, crafter, and light-hearted photographer. She owns a 4,000-square-foot home decor shop and newly launched online shop {with her mother and sister} called Grandiflora HOME. She also sells her work in three different shops via Etsy. You can find out more by visiting her blog, *trishabrinkdesign.blogspot.com*.

Trisha resides in Lynden, Washington.

Trisha's Ice Cream Cozy

Ever get a craving for ice cream when it isn't sweltering outside? Yeah, me too! Well here is the answer to those frigid finger problems: Make an Ice Cream Cozy!

Find a wool sweater that has seen better days {at least 80% wool; 100% wool works best}, wash in very hot water, and let dry {this process is called felting; it allows you to cut the sweater into pieces without it unravelling}. Next, cut sleeves off of the sweater. Continue cutting sleeves into approximately 3" inch "rings." This measurement will depend on how much the sweater has shrunk and on the circumference of the ice cream cup you will add the cozy to.

Take your time selecting various decorative odds and ends such as pieces of old granny square afghans, self-covering buttons, scrap fabric, or anything somewhat soft to the touch. Sitch and attach items to the sweater sleeve ring. Voilá — a festive frost-free way to hold on to a single-serve ice cream treat!

Trisha's Lemon Pistachio Cranberry Tarts

Makes 12 tarts

- 2 **cups heavy cream**
- 1 **{14 oz.} can sweetened condensed milk**
- 3 **TB. salted butter, melted**
- 1 **{3.4 oz} box instant pistachio pudding**
- **Juice of 2 fresh lemons**
- ½ **cup dried cranberries**
- ½ **cup pistachios, roasted, salted & shelled**
- 12 **ready-made mini graham cracker pies/tart crusts**
- **Garnish: mint sprigs, cranberries, pistachios, or sprinkles**

1. In large bowl, whip heavy cream with handheld mixer until stiff peaks form, about 5 minutes. Set aside.

2. In separate bowl whisk together sweetened condensed milk, salted butter, instant pistachio pudding, and juice of 2 fresh lemons.

3. Add dried cranberries and pistachios to pudding mix; mix well.

4. With rubber spatula, fold pudding mixture into whipped cream. Combine well.

5. Gently scoop mixture into mini graham cracker pies or tart crusts and freeze 1-2 hours or until set.

6. Garnish tarts with mint sprigs, cranberries, pistachios, or sprinkles.

LEMON PISTACHIO CRANBERRY

Handheld

{perfectly sized treats to hold in your hands to eat; no spoon required}

Go ahead grab onto one of these treats and be a kid again!

Ice Cream Surprise Treats

A sweet surprise is hidden inside these jimmie-covered ice cream treats … mini chocolate bars! How clever to add a soft-centered chocolate bar onto the stick before filling the individual cups with soft vanilla ice cream.

Makes 6 cups

- 6 mini soft-centered chocolate bars
- 1½ cups vanilla ice cream, softened
  Assorted bright-colored jimmie sprinkles
- 6 Popsicle sticks
- 6 {5 oz.} mini paper cups

1. Push Popsicle sticks into each mini candy bar.

2. Add vanilla ice cream into large bowl approximately ¼ cup of ice cream per treat. Stir to soften.

3. Making 1 treat at a time, add 1 large spoonful of ice cream to bottom of paper cup. Add mini candy bar sticks, being careful not to push all the way to bottom of cup or else candy bar will not be completely covered by ice cream.

4. Keeping the stick very straight, add additional ice cream all around until cup is almost full. Do not fill to top rim, as you will need an edge to help peel cup away once frozen. Make sure to press ice cream down as you go to avoid air pocket holes in finished treats.

5. Put immediately into freezer, making sure sticks are straight. Freeze until frozen solid, at least 4 hours or overnight.

6. Once frozen, remove from freezer 1 at a time {they melt fast}. Have bright colored sprinkles out on a large plate ready to roll treats in.

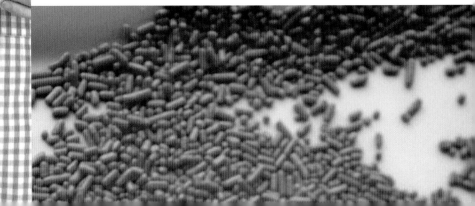

Apron to a Bag ... It is that Easy!

To make an over-the-shoulder bag for carrying to the market, all you need is a little finished apron, which can be easily found at your local thrift store for next to nothing.

Take your apron and fold it in half, right sides together. Stitch up the side and across bottom of the apron with a sewing machine. Leave top open. Turn right side out, and press. The apron ties can be lengthened or shortened to tie over your shoulder. What could be easier? What could be sweeter?

wasn't that easy?

Easy Chocolate Ice Cream Sandwiches

A fast and easy ice cream treat made from store-bought cookies and chocolate ice cream. Dip them in chocolate or leave plain ... it's up to you.

Makes 12 sandwiches

- 24 square shortbread cookies, plain/1 side dipped in chocolate {any square or rectangle cookies can be used}
- 2–2½ cups chocolate ice cream/any other flavour
- Hard Shell Covering/melted chocolate for dipping {see recipe on page 120}
- Sprinkles
- Parchment paper

1. Line 8" x 8" pan with parchment paper.

2. For bottom layer, lay down 12 shortbread cookies side by side.

NOTE: If using chocolate-dipped cookies, have chocolate side facing up.

3. Soften chocolate ice cream or any other flavour and spread evenly over cookie layer.

4. Place 1 cookie on top of each row as a guide for future placement of top cookies; bottom cookies and top cookies should line up evenly when slicing up sandwiches. Put into freezer to harden slightly.

5. Once ice cream is firmed up but not solid, place rest of the cookies on top; pushing firmly into place. Put back into freezer until frozen solid, at least 4 hours.

6. Once frozen, remove from pan easily by lifting up parchment paper. Slice into individual sandwiches; for easy slicing, thaw slightly.

7. Put individual sandwiches back into freezer to firm up.

8. Dip half of sandwich in Hard Shell Covering or melted chocolate, then into sprinkles; return to freezer to harden and until ready to eat.

chocolate ice cream sandwiches

high on
gingham

Sweet Little Cupcake Liner Packages

- Waxed paper strips, 5" x 12"
- Cupcake liners
- Sewing machine
- String or ribbon, for decorating

1. Fold waxed paper in half for a fold line guide in center; unfold.

2. Flatten out cupcake liners and center each liner on top of unfolded waxed paper. Using a sewing machine, sew liners onto waxed paper.

3. Fold waxed paper in half; liner should sit half on one side and half on the other side of waxed paper. Machine stitch up both sides of wax paper, leaving top end open to add your treat.

4. Decorate by tying a bow with string or ribbon if desired.

finding the quiet center of our lives

A Sweet Treat on a Stick {Rice Cereal Treats}

These adorable little treats take no time to whip up using a traditional Rice Cereal Treat recipe.

Makes 6 to 8 treats

RICE CEREAL TREATS

½ cup butter, plus extra for moulds
4 cups mini marshmallows
1½ tsp. vanilla extract
6 cups rice cereal
6 Popsicle moulds
6 Popsicle sticks

1. Melt butter and mini marshmallows over low heat in large pan. Remove from heat. Stir in vanilla extract; once vanilla is evenly stirred in, add rice cereal. Mix well.

2. Lightly butter inside of each Popsicle mould, and fill with cereal mixture; pressing firmly.

3. Insert Popsicle sticks. Let harden a few hours or overnight. The firmer the cereal gets, the easier the treats are to remove from moulds; a gentle tug on the stick is all that should be needed.

DECORATING

2 cups pink candy melts/chocolate
Cake decorating sprinkles
Cupcake liners

1. Melt pink candy melts or chocolate over simmering hot water or in microwave {see package for instructions}.

2. Dip top of Rice Cereal Treats into melted candy or chocolate. It may be easier to spread on with a spatula if using candy melts. Immediately sprinkle each treat with cake decorating sprinkles; it is best to do each one individually, as once melts harden, sprinkles will not stick.

3. Make a pretty paper bottom by slicing a slit into the bottom of each cupcake liner; just large enough for stick to slide onto.

Peanut Butter Bar Ice Cream Sandwiches on a Stick

These fat, chunky sandwich bars have vanilla ice cream sandwiched between 2 peanut butter squares, are dipped in milk chocolate, and are rolled in crushed peanuts.

Makes 6 or 8 bars, depending on size

PEANUT BUTTER BARS

- ½ cup butter
- ½ cup sugar
- ½ cup brown sugar
- ½ cup peanut butter
- 1 egg
- 1½ tsp. vanilla extract
- 1 cup flour
- ½ tsp. baking soda
- Parchment paper

1. Preheat oven to 375°F.
2. Cream butter with sugars. Add peanut butter and beat well.
3. Beat in egg and vanilla extract; blend in flour and baking soda.
4. Press mixture into 9" x 13" pan lined with parchment paper.
5. Bake 12–15 minutes, or until lightly golden.
6. Let cool completely before assembling ice cream sandwiches.

ASSEMBLING SANDWICHES

- Peanut Butter Bars
- 2–2½ cups vanilla ice cream, softened
- Chunky Popsicle sticks
- 1 package milk chocolate chips
- 1 cup peanuts, crushed
- Parchment paper

1. Remove Peanut Butter Bars from pan and cut off crust with pizza cutter or sharp knife; cut into 2 equal slabs.
2. Line small pan {8" x 8" or smaller} with parchment paper. Put half of bar slab in pan, and smooth ice cream evenly over top. Place other bar slab on top of vanilla ice cream layer; press firmly. Wrap tightly and freeze until solid, at least 4 hours or overnight.
3. Remove from pan and cut into squares with very sharp knife. Insert Popsicle stick into bottom of each sandwich bar and freeze to firm up for easy dipping.
4. Melt milk chocolate chips and put in small container deep enough to cover entire bar. Dip bar in chocolate and immediately roll in peanuts. Place in freezer to firm up before eating.

delectable *delicious* delightful

Caramel *Marshmallow* Cookie Treats

Caramel Marshmallow Cookie Treats

These treats can be made 2 ways: If you can't find caramel bits you can make your own caramel. {I prefer to make my own caramel, as this recipe is delicious and easy!} These sweet treats are made even sweeter when you serve them on a stick.

Makes 6 to 8 bars on sticks

	Butter, to grease pan
4½	graham crackers
1⅓	cups caramel bits/Homemade Caramel
2	TB. whole milk
½	cup pretzels, crushed
½	cup white chocolate chips
½	cup salted peanuts
½	cup mini marshmallows
1	cup milk/semi-sweet chocolate chips
	Parchment paper
	Popsicle sticks

1. Line loaf pan with parchment paper; grease with butter.

2. Place graham crackers on bottom of prepared pan, cutting to fit if necessary.

3. Melt caramel bits or Homemade Caramel with whole milk in microwave; stir until completely melted and smooth. Pour over graham crackers and top with pretzels, white chocolate chips, salted peanuts, and mini marshmallows.

4. Melt milk or semi-sweet chocolate chips and spread over top evenly.

5. Let cool completely in fridge before cutting into bars and adding Popsicle sticks. Put back in fridge until ready to eat, as caramel can get runny.

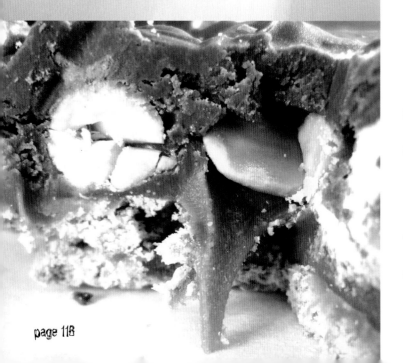

Homemade Caramel

Makes about ¾ cups

- ½ cup butter
- ½ cup brown sugar
- 2 TB. light corn syrup
- ½ cup sweetened condensed milk
- 1 tsp. vanilla extract

1. Combine butter, brown sugar, light corn syrup, and sweetneded condensed milk in saucepan. Bring to a boil, reduce heat, and continue to stir for 5 minutes; letting mixture boil while stirring.

2. Remove from heat and add vanilla extract; stir with wooden spoon for another 3 minutes.

Just for **today** ...
give **yourself** the **gift**
of **time** to **nurture**
your **spirits**.

Homemade Drumsticks

We love these in my home because there are so many different combinations you can make. All you need to start are basic sugar cones, ice cream, and hard shell chocolate; then just add any other treat into the mix to make these drumsticks extra special and personalized.

Makes 1 cup

HARD SHELL COVERING

> 1 cup coconut oil {adds a nice flavour to the chocolate}
>
> 2 cups chocolate, broken into pieces {I prefer good-quality dark chocolate, but milk or semi-sweet will work just as well}
>
> Pinch of sea salt

1. Melt coconut oil in saucepan over low heat.

2. Add chocolate and stir until melted and well-blended.

3. Remove from heat and add sea salt.

4. Store in jar or squeeze bottle. It will harden once cool, so just reheat when ready to use.

NOTE: When poured on cold ice cream, it will harden immediately.

SUGAR CONES

> Sugar cones
>
> Hard Shell Covering/store-bought hard shell chocolate
>
> Waxed paper

1. Keep cones plain, or add Hard Shell Covering or store-bought hard shell chocolat to the inside of each cone; just pour chocolate inside cone and swirl it around to coat. Pour more chocolate into cone base for an extra treat.

2. Once hard shell is dry, wrap cones with waxed paper {leaving a few extra inches above the cones' top}. This allows the drumstick to have a few inches of ice cream above the cone once waxed paper is removed.

the start of something good

VANILLA PEANUT DRUMSTICK

> **Sugar Cones**
>
> **Simple Vanilla Bean Ice Cream (see recipe on page 10}**
>
> **Hard Shell Covering/store-bought hard shell chocolate**
>
> **Peanuts, crushed**

1. Fill prepared Sugar Cone with Simple Vanilla Bean Ice Cream, making sure to fill about 1" above cones' rim {this is why the waxed paper liners are needed}. Smooth top out evenly.

2. Stand cones upright in freezer to harden.

3. Once ice cream has hardened, add Hard Shell Covering and crushed peanuts.

4. Store in freezer until ready to eat; serve with Cone from Vintage Wallpaper Samples.

VARIATIONS: To make …

- Strawberry Malt Drumsticks, fill cones with strawberry ice cream and top with Hard Shell Covering and crushed and whole malt balls.

- Coffee Wafer Drumsticks, fill cones with alternating layers of coffee ice cream and pieces of a wafer-type chocolate bar. Top with Hard Shell Covering and more crushed wafer pieces.

Vanilla Peanut

Strawberry Malt

Coffee Waffer

Cone Covers from Vintage Wallpaper Samples

I just adore the look of vintage wallpaper, so I thought, "Why not use some to wrap around my drumsticks?" The only thing was that the wallpaper was thick and some of my samples had paste on the back. So, I came up with the idea of color photocopying the wallpaper samples onto normal paper. Then I made the cone covers from the photocopied pages. I love the look!

Strawberry Shortcakes on a Stick

These sweet little bars have layers of puréed strawberries in-between Simple Vanilla Bean Ice Cream, are dipped in a vanilla coating, and are sprinkled with crushed vanilla and strawberry ice wafers.

Makes 6, depending on size of moulds

- 2 cups fresh/frozen unsweetened strawberries
- ½ cup sugar
- 2 cups Simple Vanilla Bean Ice Cream, softened {see recipe on page 10}
- ¼ cup vanilla ice wafers, crushed
- ¾ cup strawberry ice wafers, crushed
- 2 cups vanilla melting chips/wafers
- Popsicle moulds or little paper cups
- Popsicle sticks

1. Purée fresh or frozen strawberries in blender, and add sugar.

2. In bottom of each Popsicle mould or paper cup, add 1 layer of berry purée and 1 layer of softened Simple Vanilla Bean Ice Cream; freeze until firm.

3. Remove from freezer and top with another layer of purée followed by ice cream {if you want an additional strawberry layer, leave just enough room for last layer of purée to be added after these layers have been hardened in freezer}. Freeze at least 2 hours, or more.

4. Remove from moulds {you may have to dip into hot water; or, if in paper cups, paper can be peeled off}, then pop back into freezer to harden.

5. Combine vanilla ice and strawberry ice wafers in bowl.

6. Melt vanilla melting chips or wafers according to directions on package, and dip each bar, one at a time, to coat evenly. Once dipped, immediately cover with mixture of crushed wafers.

7. Freeze to harden and until ready to serve.

Ice Cream Cone Cards

These little cards or tags are ever so easy and can be made in no time.

Scrap piece of fabric for cone

White cardstock for card

Little pieces of wool/yarn

A little bit of pretty paper for heart

White glue, clear-drying

1. Cut out cone shape from fabric piece, and glue onto card.

2. Shape wool or yarn into spiral shape and glue on top of cone.

3. Add a little paper heart to cone with glue.

sprucing up the **vanilla**

Paper Doily Ice Cream Cones

Start by taking a pretty pink cone {or any color} and adding a paper doily cut in half around its base with double-sided tape. Then add a scoop of vanilla ice cream, a pretty candy melt, and sprinkles. Could anything be more charming?

Pinwheel Cookies on a Stick

These little cookies are just as darling without the stick and sprinkles. Just fill up a little bag and give them to those you love.

Makes 12 to 14 cookies

1	cup butter
1½	cups sugar
1½	tsp. baking powder
½	tsp. salt
1	egg
2	tsp. vanilla extract
2½	cups flour
	Pink paste food coloring
	Nonpareil sprinkles {if desired}
	Dab of icing
	Cookie sticks
	Little paper heart

Swirls and twirls of pink

Pinwheel cookies

1. Beat butter until light and fluffy; add sugar and continue to beat until well-incorporated. Add baking powder, salt, egg, and vanilla extract; mix well until all ingredients are combined.

2. Add flour a little bit at a time, mixing well after each addition. You may have to stir the last little bit of flour in by hand or by kneading on the countertop.

3. Divide dough in half. Add a few drops of pink food coloring to 1 portion of dough, kneading color into dough to get desired shade. Remember, just a little coloring goes a long way. Wrap dough balls with waxed paper and refrigerate until firm and easy to roll, approximately 1 hour.

4. Lightly flour surface and roll each dough ball into rectangle shape {¼" thick}. If dough sticks, roll between 2 pieces of waxed paper. Trim both rectangles to equal size, place 1 rectangle on top of other, and press down gently to seal.

5. Tightly roll up dough, starting with the long end, into jelly-roll shape; smooth dough as you go.

6. Cut roll in half; this will make it easier to roll into nonpareil sprinkles. Take each half, and roll into large plate of sprinkles; press down firmly, as sprinkles do not like to stick. Roll several times if necessary. Tightly cover rolls with waxed paper and refrigerate 2–4 hours before baking. Once waxed paper is around rolls, press around edges of each roll firmly, as this will help sprinkles to stick.

7. Preheat oven to 375ºF.

8. Using a sharp knife, cut roll into ¼–¾" slices {thick enough to add a stick, thinner for a cookie without a stick}. Insert a stick into each cookie and bake on cookie sheet lined with parchment paper for 10–12 minutes or until lightly brown. Cool on cookie sheet for about 2 minutes before removing to wire rack to cool completely.

NOTE: Not all sprinkles can be baked in the oven. Make sure you test your sprinkles first if you are unsure. Usually nonpareils are fine, but some of the fancier ones just for cake decorating will melt in the heat.

9. Add little paper heart onto center of each cookie with a dab of icing {can be easily removed when ready to eat}.

Just for today ...
be in it with all your heart.

Meet My Friend Jacqueline

Jacqueline Low loves to create; her functional and whimsical items evolve around cuteness and love.

Her passion for art comes in the form of sewing and embroidery. Jacqueline was inspired by her babysitter, Granny Mary. Granny Mary used to sew cute little dresses for her Cabbage Patch Kid from leftover vintage cotton fabrics. Jacqueline remembers sitting around Granny Mary's sewing machine as she worked magic on those wonderful fabrics, turning them into something lovely and useful. Jacqueline states, "Granny Mary showered me with such a love of creating that I blossomed into an artsy, crafty kid."

Visit Jacqueline's adorable crafty blog at *jqlinesocuteithurts.typepad.com*.

Jacqueline's Red Bean Ice Cream Bars

One of my favorite childhood traditional Chinese desserts is red bean ice cream. My papa loved to cook for the family; it was 1 of his specialities.

Makes 4 to 6 bars

- ½ cup sugar
- 3 egg yolks
- 1 cup whole milk
- *1 cup red bean paste
- *½ cup semi-whole red beans
- 1½ cups heavy cream
- Ice cream moulds

*Found in the Asian section of your local Supermarket. If you are unable to find red beans, kidney beans can be substituted.

1. Beat sugar and egg yolks together in medium bowl until pale yellow.

2. Bring whole milk to a boil in medium saucepan and remove from heat. Whisk into egg mixture and pour entire mixture back into saucepan. Stir constantly over medium-low heat with a whisk until custard thickens {about 5 minutes}, making sure to scrape bottom of pan.

3. Strain custard into a clean bowl. Mix in red bean paste and semi-whole red beans; stir in heavy cream.

4. Cover and refrigerate overnight before processing, according to ice cream maker's instructions.

5. Pour into ice cream moulds and freeze until firm.

Just for today ...
try someting new.

Meet my Friend Torie

Torie Jayne is a fashion designer by day, and a baker, crafter, and enthusiastic wannabe interior designer by night, with a little gardening on the side! Her personal style is a little bit vintage, a dash of modern, and heavily color palette driven. Torie's creative blog features pretty decorated gluten-free baking, shops she loves, inspiring images, and seasonal dessert tables. Visit her blog at *toriejayne.blogspot.com*.

Torie's Eton Mess Ice Cream Cone

A sprinkled cone filled with a creamy vanilla ice cream swirled with strawberry sauce, and topped with a piped meringue swirl.

Makes 4 cups

ETON MESS ICE CREAM

    3 cups fresh strawberries

    ½ cup sugar

    3 egg yolks

    1 cup whole milk

    1 cup heavy cream

    1 tsp. vanilla extract

    2 cups Heart-Shaped Meringue Cookies, crushed; plus extra for decorating cones {see recipe on page 44}

1. Blend fresh strawberries with ¼ cup sugar, so you are left with a sugary purée; place in fridge. Place a second empty bowl in the fridge to cool.

2. Beat egg yolks, and place in a medium saucepan with milk and ¼ cup sugar on medium heat; stir until just boiling. Pour mixture into chilled bowl and, when cool, place in refrigerator for up to 3 hours, stirring every half hour or so.

3. When mixture is cool, stir in heavy cream, vanilla extract, Heart-Shaped Meringue Cookies, and strawberry/sugar mixture.

4. Transfer mixture to ice cream maker, and follow as per your machine's instructions.

PRETTY CONE WRAPPERS

- **Cone template**
- **Pretty cardstock**
- **Double-sided tape**

1. Use template as reference to cut full size cone shape.

2. Place template on pretty cardstock, and trace around edges with pencil. Cut out template carefully.

3. Roll wrapper into cone shape and, using double-sided tape, fix in shape. Place waffle cone into cone holder.

SPRINKLED CONES

- **Pink chocolate candy melts**
- **Waffle cones**
- **White sprinkles**

1. Melt chocolate candy melts per packet's instructions.

2. Dip open end of waffle cone into melted chocolate, and swirl so all edges are covered in pink chocolate.

3. Immediately dip candy-covered cone into bowl of sprinkles until candy is covered in white sprinkles; leave to dry.

4. Fill cone with 1 scoop of Eton Mess Ice Cream, and dip into remaining crushed meringue.

Just for **today** ...
thank a **friend** with
something **special**.

Simple

{not elaborate or complicated to make; easy peasy}

Shhhhhh ... don't let anyone how easy these desserts are to whip up; they will think you have been slaving over them for hours. Fast and easy but oh so pretty.

neapolitan ice cream cake
{best dressed award}

Neapolitan Ice Cream Cake

It really does not get any simpler than this! All you need is one square carton of Neapolitan ice cream. Cut the carton off the ice cream, and refreeze until ice cream is hard. Melt a good-quality chocolate, and pour chocolate over the top of frozen ice cream, letting it run down the sides. Quickly pile on any topping you like; I used cubed strawberry ice cream wafers and chocolate bar pieces. Refreeze until topping is set. Slice and enjoy!

Orange Cream Milkshakes

This is a family favorite. Adding a scoop of vanilla ice cream or orange sorbet just before serving makes it kind of like a milkshake float.

Makes 2 shakes

- 5 scoops vanilla ice cream
- ½ cup orange juice with pulp
- ½ cup whole milk
- ⅓ cup orange juice concentrate, plus extra to taste
- 2 scoops orange sorbet/vanilla ice cream {to be added after blending}
- Fresh orange slices for garnish

1. In blender, mix vanilla ice cream, orange juice, whole milk, and orange juice concentrate; blend well.

2. Pour into glasses, add a scoop of orange sorbet or vanilla ice cream, and garnish with fresh orange slices. Serve with a tall spoon.

milkshake
orange cream

Just for today ...
keep it fresh and
keep it simple.

don't forget

to

play

Ice Cream Pizza

This is such a fun activity for any type of get-together. Make and bake individual cookie crusts ahead of time so that all you have left to do is gather up the yummy toppings and ice cream, sit back, and watch the fun begin.

Its fun for everyone to make their own individual mini pizza, but you could easily have 1 big pizza and give everyone their own section to create.

SUGAR COOKIE PIZZA CRUST

To make this super simple, just use ready-made sugar cookie dough or make it yourself with this easy recipe.

Makes 1 large pizza or 4 individual-sized pizzas

- ½ cup butter, softened
- ¾ cup sugar
- 1 egg
- 1 tsp. vanilla extract
- 1¼ cups flour
- 1 tsp. cream of tartar
- ½ tsp. baking soda
- ¼ tsp. salt

1. Preheat oven to 350ºF.
2. In large bowl, cream together butter and sugar until smooth; beat in egg and vanilla extract.
3. In separate bowl, combine flour, cream of tartar, baking soda, and salt; stir into butter mixture until blended.
4. Press dough into ungreased pizza pan or 4 individual-sized pans.
5. Bake 8–10 minutes or until lightly browned. Cool completely before using.

ASSEMBLING ICE CREAM PIZZA

If making these for a party, have guests make them first thing, as they need to firm up in the freezer before serving.

> Vanilla ice cream/your favorite flavour
>
> Sugar Cookie Pizza Crust
>
> Variety of sauces: chocolate, butterscotch, caramel, strawberry, etc.
>
> Oodles of fun toppings: nuts, candy, fruit, gummies, chocolate chips, etc.

1. Soften vanilla ice cream so that it can be easily spread on top of Sugar Cookie Pizza Crust. Cover crust completely with ice cream.

2. Working fast, spread sauces and toppings over ice cream.

3. Freeze until firm, at least 2 hours or longer. Remove from freezer and cut with pizza cutter or sharp knife.

NOTE: Serve immediately; leftovers can be covered and refrozen.

Simple Sprinkle Candles

Using any clear glass container, just add a candle and cake sprinkles — simple, easy, and fun.

S'more Bar Milkshakes

S'mores are the ultimate camping food. No camping trip is complete without this oozy, gooey, chocolate treat. We are a "true blue" camping family; every summer we pile into our jam-packed van filled with our tenting gear.

Our first stop is to buy s'more supplies — chocolate bars, large marshmallows, and graham crackers. These milkshakes are a drinkable version of the classic s'more bars.

s'more bar milkshake

Just for today ...
do not wish to be
anything but what
you are.

Makes 2 large shakes or 4 small ones

- 1 cup whole milk
- 5–6 cups vanilla ice cream
- 1 cup marshmallow creme

  Hot Fudge Sauce
  {see recipe on page 157}

  Sweetened whipped cream

- 1 graham cracker, crushed
- 2 large marshmallows for 2 milkshakes/4 for 4 milkshakes, toasted in broiler for decoration {put in broiler until toasted ... watch carefully!}

1. Combine whole milk, vanilla ice cream, and marshmallow creme in blender until thick and smooth. If mixture is too thin, add more ice cream.

2. In large glass; add 2 tablespoons or so of Hot Fudge Sauce; add enough milkshake mixture to fill glass half full. Add more fudge sauce and top off with more milkshake mixture.

3. Add sweetened whipped cream, a drizzle of fudge sauce, graham crackers, and a toasted marshmallow.

Hankie Apron

This adorable apron was given to me as a sweet gift from my friend, Krishana. I knew when I saw it that I just had to include it in my book.

Its simplicity makes it very easy to make; just sew 4 large dainty hankies together and add an extra-wide satin ribbon for the tie. Add a darling little embellishment or just leave as is.

You can find other adorable ideas on Krishana's lovely blog, Aurora Blythe, *aurora-blythe.blogspot.ca.*

perfectlypretty pressies

Pretty Hankie Wrapping Paper

I love sweet hankies and have collected many different patterns. Sometimes I will use my hankies to wrap little gifts in, but there are times when I don't want to give away a special hankie. I will then make colored copies of them by simply using a photocopier to copy the sweet hankie prints onto paper. I then use this paper to wrap up little gifts; this way I can also keep my favorite hankie.

Cupcake Liner Garland

Create a sweet little garland suitable for any occasion just by using your favorite cupcake liners and twine.

Flatten cupcake liners, fold them into a fan shape, and tie them onto a piece of baker's twine, making sure they are evenly spaced. Different-sized liners can be used as well.

cupcake liner garland

Fancy Up Your ...

This is such an adorable and simple way to fancy up an ice cream sandwich or those plain slippers of yours. All you need is melted chocolate and sprinkles or 2 pieces of cotton lace {approximately 30" long for each flower}, some thread, and a needle.

For each sandwich, dip in chocolate and roll in sprinkles. For each flower, run a gathering stitch through one side of the lace, leaving a long piece of thread at either end. Gently pull thread through lace to create an even gather on 1 side. Roll up lace to create a rose-like flower and attach to the top of each slipper.

Oodles of Fruit Banana Split

What could be better than a classic banana split to share between friends?

The bananas in the original banana splits were unpeeled until the creator realized that customers preferred their bananas peeled.

Makes 1 banana split

- 1 large banana, peeled & cut in half lengthwise
- 1 large scoop vanilla, chocolate & strawberry ice cream
- Fresh strawberries, sliced
- Fresh pineapple, cut into chunks
- Chocolate pieces
- Sweetened whipped cream

Put all ingredients into a large, long dish in the traditional banana split fashion, and enjoy!

for you with love

easy as... 1. 2. 3.

Just for today ... too much is never enough.

Mini Ice Cream Cups

Mini little jam jars are perfect for holding these yummy little afterschool treats.

Just layer ice cream {any flavour} with nuts and a favorite sauce. I use vanilla, peanuts, and hot fudge or butterscotch sauce.

It is so much fun to open the freezer and have these little nibbles ready to snack on.

Sprucing up the **Vanilla**

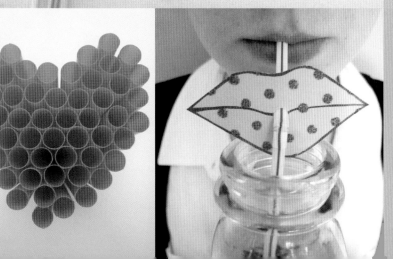

Frothy Chocolate Milkshakes

This thin shake is more like a rich, yummy glass of frothy cold chocolate milk.

Makes 4 shakes

- 3 cups whole milk
- 6 TB. chocolate powdered drink mix
- 7 ice cubes
- ½ cup chocolate ice cream
- Chocolate sprinkles

1. Mix whole milk, powder drink mix, and ice cubes together in a blender until smooth.

2. Add chocolate ice cream and pulse briefly; you do not want ice cream to blend completely.

3. Top with chocolate sprinkles.

NOTE: For an alternative and fun float-type milkshake, add a scoop of ice cream to glass first and top with blended chocolate milk mixture.

frothy
chocolate
shake

Paper Lip Straw Toppers

What a fun way to dress up your straws. Using decorative cardstock paper, cut out lip shapes. Trace around edges to define, and punch out a hole for your straw. Bendy straws work the best.

Meet Ali, Daughter Number 1

Ali is my smart cookie; she can always be found in the kitchen cooking up health conscious meals for her and her husband. She is the healthiest eater of the family, but does have her dad's sweet tooth, so once in a while I can find her with her hands in the cookie jar.

Her simple Oatmeal Cookie Milkshakes are deliciously yummy and can be whipped up fast when using store-bought oatmeal cookies.

Ali's Oatmeal Cookie Milkshakes

Makes 2 large shakes

- 2 oatmeal cookies, 1 crushed
- 1½ cups vanilla ice cream
- ⅔ cup milk
- ½ tsp. cinnamon

1. Prepare glasses by wetting rim of glass with water, and dipping rim in cookie crumbs.

2. In blender, mix remaining ingredients until smooth. Pour into prepared glasses.

3. Slice remaining oatmeal cookie and place on side of glass.

Meet Sydney, Daughter Number 3

Sydney is my creative ballerina. She is always thinking outside the box, so it doesn't surprise me that she came up with this creative recipe.

One of her favorite summer treats are store-bought ice cream sandwiches. She took one Neapolitan ice cream sandwich, cut it up into strips to line a mason jar, and then added extra ice cream and toppings to create this simply adorable ice cream treat. Top it with whipped cream and a candle and get ready to sing happy birthday!

Sydney's Ice Cream Sandwiches in a Jar

You can create your own individual treat by adding your favorite toppings or ice cream.

Makes 1 jar

- 1 Neapolitan ice cream sandwich
  Hot Fudge Sauce {see recipe on page 157}
  Strawberry ice cream/any other flavour
  Sweetened whipped cream for garnish
- 1 very small Mason jar

1. Cut ice cream sandwich into strips to fit around Mason jar {7 even pieces}.

2. Add 1 tablespoon or so of Hot Fudge Sauce into center hole, and then top with a layer of strawberry ice cream or any other flavour.

3. Cover with more fudge sauce; tap bottom of jar on table to settle fudge down through sides of sandwiches. Add lid and freeze until solid, at least 2 hours or overnight.

4. Just before serving, top with sweetened whipped cream.

ice cream **sandwiches** in a jar

Adorn

{to enhance by decorating or by making more attractive; adding a bit of pizazz}

It is up to you; add a little or a lot.

a bowl full of *sprinkles*
...utterly irresistible

Sprinkles

I think sprinkles were invented to make the world a happier place. I know that every time I look at these little bits of sweetness, I catch myself smiling.

Sprinkles are little candy decorations that are sprinkled over a surface. I think I tend to sprinkle them more than most people do.

Even the names for these little guys are adorable! Sprinkles can be known as jimmies, hundreds and thousands, nonpareils, confetti, dragees, sanding sugar, crystal sugar, and pearl sugar ... just to name a few.

Ice cream and sprinkles are a match made in heaven; all you need is a few sprinkles to make your ice cream happy. If you want to get fancy, you can even make your own {see recipe on page 11}. So what are you waiting for? Get sprinkling!

sprucing up the **vanilla**

Ice Cream St

White Chocolate Stir Spoons

We love these! So easy to make and so much fun, and perfect for stirring up your hot chocolate or for giving as gifts.

All you need are some plastic spoons {or regular silverware if you want to get fancy}, chocolate or candy melts {any flavour}, and sprinkles.

Melt the chocolate or melts and pour a little into each spoon. Quickly add sprinkles of your choice and let set until hardened; store in refrigerator.

Dipped Chocolate Bar Pieces

These are just what a simple bowl of ice cream needs to spruce it up. Or, add these pieces around the bottom of your ice cream cake to make it extra adorable.

Dip chocolate bar pieces into melted white chocolate or pretty-colored candy melts, and add sprinkles. Metallic dragees are so festive to use in pretty pastel colors. Refrigerate immediately. Because the dip is hot, the chocolate on the bar will melt, so you have to work fast.

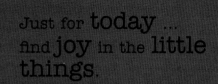

Sprinkle Melts

Custom make these melts in any color combination to coordinate with whatever ice cream celebration you have going on; perfect for cake decorating too.

Start with candy melts of any color. Cut little pieces of parchment paper, big enough for 3 melts.

Put melts on paper to form a triangle, but not too close together as you do not want them to melt together. Microwave about 35 seconds. If you do more than 3 melts at a time, they will not melt evenly. Remove from microwave, and sprinkle the sprinkles over tops of melts; let cool completely before removing from paper.

Flower Melts

These look like little pansies and are so perfect for decorating a spring ice cream cake.

Using candy melts of any color; lay 3 close together on a little piece of parchment paper to a form flower shape. Microwave for 35 seconds, remove, and add some sprinkles and a candied flower to the center of each candy melt flower. Let cool completely before removing from paper.

Strawberry Dippers

Sprinkles can be put on anything, so why not try a fresh strawberry? A perfect addition to anything ice cream.

Make sure you clean and dry berries completely before dipping them into melted candy melts or chocolate and then into a bowl of sprinkles. Here you are allowed to double dip!

Raspberry Chippers

Raspberry and chocolate are a favorite taste combination! You can create an adorable effect without a lot of work. Just clean and dry fresh raspberries and add 1 chocolate chip, white or dark, into each center with the curl part facing upward. So yummy to eat just as a snack.

gummy shish kabobs

Gummy Shish Kabobs

Everyone loves gummies, and what fun it is
use them to make shish kabobs! Perfect for
a child's birthday party. You can even color
coordinate kabobs because the variety of
gummies are endless.

it's bloomin' marvellous

dirt never tasted this *good*

Ice Cream Flowerpots

Grow your own gummies in these flowerpots. All you need are a few mini terracotta flowerpots {large enough to fit individual-sized ice cream cartons, which can be found at most grocery stores} and chalkboard paint. Chalkboard paint comes in a variety of colors; mine is teal.

Paint flowerpots {2 coats} and let dry completely overnight. Assemble flowerpots just before serving: Put ice cream containers into pots and cover with crushed chocolate wafer crumbs; this will be the dirt. Add Gummy Shish Kabobs {see recipe on page 153} and serve.

Sugared Flowers

These little guys are so easy to make; they just take a few days to dry. You must use only edible flowers such as pansies, violets, or chamomile flowers.

Cut flower stems short with just enough room to hold onto flower as you work. Dilute pasteurized liquid egg whites with small amount of water. With a tiny paintbrush, brush egg white wash onto entire flower surface. Quickly, before wash dries, sprinkle with superfine sugar {regular sugar is too coarse}. Let dry in a warm place up to 4 days, turning regularly. Store in a dry place up to 30 days.

let a *joy* keep you
Carl Sandburg

Chocolate Sauce

Makes 3 cups

- ¾ cup unsweetened Dutch-process cocoa powder, sifted
- 2 cups water
- 2 cups sugar
- Pinch of salt
- ¾ cup dark bittersweet chocolate, coarsely chopped
- 1 TB. vanilla extract

1. Mix unsweetened Dutch-process cocoa powder with water and bring to a boil over medium heat, stirring constantly.

2. Stir in sugar and salt; let simmer about 2 minutes. Remove from heat.

3. Stir in dark bittersweet chocolate until melted completely; add vanilla extract.

4. To obtain a very smooth, thin, syrupy-type sauce, pour through sieve into large bowl. Let cool completely before storing in airtight container. Keep in refrigerator up to 2 months.

White Chocolate Sauce

Makes 2 cups

- 1 cup heavy cream
- 2 cups white chocolate chips/white baking chocolate
- 1 tsp. vanilla extract

1. Heat heavy cream in saucepan over medium heat, stirring constantly.

2. Remove from heat and add white chocolate chips or white baking chocolate; whisk until smooth. It may take a while for chocolate to dissolve completely. Stir in vanilla extract.

3. Let cool to room temperature. Store in refrigerator in airtight container up to 2 weeks.

Hot Fudge Sauce

Makes 2 cups

- **1** cup heavy cream
- **⅓** cup light corn syrup, plus extra if needed for consistency
- **2** cups dark bittersweet chocolate, finely chopped
- **1** tsp. vanilla extract

1. In medium saucepan, combine heavy cream and light corn syrup. Bring to a boil over medium heat, stirring constantly.

2. Remove from heat and add dark bittersweet chocolate. If too thick, adjust consistency with more corn syrup. Whisk in vanilla extract.

3. Let cool completely before serving. Store in refrigerator in airtight container up to 2 weeks.

4. Warm just before serving on ice cream.

Caramel Sauce

Makes 2½ cups

- **2** cups sugar
- **½** cup water
- **1½** cups heavy cream
- **1** tsp. vanilla extract
- **2** TB. unsalted butter
- Pinch of salt

1. In medium saucepan, mix together sugar and water; cook over medium heat until sugar dissolves. Bring to a boil and continue to cook without stirring. Occasionally wipe sides of pan with a spatula to prevent sugar granules from crystallizing.

2. Once sugar has caramelized and is a rich amber color, remove from heat and gradually add heavy cream. Stir until smooth. Add vanilla extract.

3. Let caramel slightly cool to warm before whisking in unsalted butter and salt.

4. Cover and refrigerate until ready to serve. Serve warm if desired. Store in refrigerator in airtight container up to 2 weeks.

Butterscotch Sauce

Butterscotch Sauce is different than Caramel Sauce because of the type of sugar used; Butterscotch Sauce uses both white and brown sugar and has a richer flavour.

Makes 1½ cups

- ½ cup unsalted butter
- ½ cup packed dark-brown sugar
- ½ cup sugar
- ¾ cup light corn syrup
- ⅓ cup heavy cream
- 1 tsp. vanilla extract

1. Melt unsalted butter in large skillet. Add sugars and light corn syrup. Boil about 2 minutes, stirring constantly.

2. Remove from heat and slowly stir in heavy cream and vanilla extract. Let cool slightly before serving. Store in refrigerator in airtight container up to 1 week. Serve warm if desired.

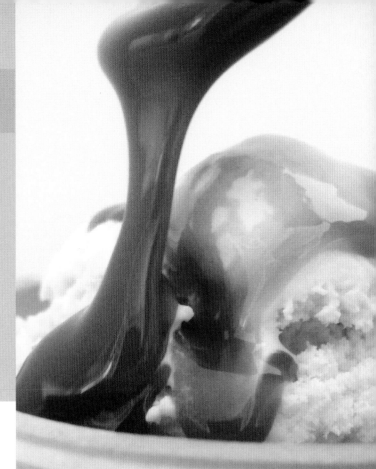

Strawberry Sauce

Makes 2 cups

- 4 cups fresh strawberries, sliced
- ¼ cup sugar, plus extra to taste
- 2 tsp. fresh lemon juice

1. Purée fresh strawberries in blender or food processor; add sugar and fresh lemon juice. Add more sugar if necessary.

2. Store in the refrigerator in airtight container up to 2 days.

Blackberry or Raspberry Sauce

Makes 1½ cups

- **2** cups fresh blackberries/raspberries
- **½** cup sugar, plus extra to taste for blackberries
- **1** TB. fresh lemon juice
- **2** tsp. cornstarch

1. Combine fresh blackberries or raspberries and sugar in saucepan over medium heat and bring to a boil, stirring often. Simmer for 3 minutes.

2. Mix together fresh lemon juice and cornstarch in small bowl until cornstarch dissolves. Add to berries and stir until thickened, about 1 minute.

3. Stir in more sugar if needed to sweeten.

4. Let cool completely or serve warm. Store in the refrigerator in airtight container up to 3 days.

Jo's Salted Caramel Ice Cream

Makes 2 cups

CARAMEL PRALINE TOPPING

   1 cup sugar

1¼ cups cream

   ½ tsp. flaky sea salt {fleur de sei or Maldon}

   ½ tsp. vanilla extract

1. Spread sugar in dry, 10" heavy skillet. Heat over medium heat, stirring with heat-proof utensil to heat sugar evenly, until it starts to melt. Stop stirring and cooking until sugar melts evenly, until it is dark amber.

2. Add cream and cook, stirring, until all of caramel has dissolved. Transfer to bowl and stir in flakey sea salt and vanilla extract. Cool to room temperature.

3. Add over ice cream.

ICE CREAM

   1 cup whole milk

   1 cup whipping cream

   ¼ cup sugar

   3 large eggs

1. Bring whole milk, whipping cream, and sugar just to a boil in small, heavy saucepan, stirring occasionally.

2. Whisk large eggs in medium bowl, then add half of hot milk mixture in a steady slow stream, whisking constantly. Pour back into saucepan and cook over medium heat, stirring constantly with a wooden spoon, until custard coats back of spoon and registers 170°F on an instant-read thermometer {do not let boil}. Pour custard through fine-mesh sieve into large bowl, and stir in cooled caramel mixture.

3. Chill custard, stirring occasionally, until very cold, about 3–6 hours. Freeze custard in ice cream maker {it will still be quite soft}, transfer to airtight container, and put in freezer to harden.

Meet My Friend Jo

My friend Jo Packham loves food — everything about food — writing about it, eating it, and the labors of working in the garden to harvest it. She believes that everyone should spend some quality time digging in the dirt; but, what she loves most of all is the creating of something unexpected with food. She has a great respect for those chefs, bakers, and foodies who imagine something new, something simple, something that changes the way a particular food or dish is enjoyed from that moment forward. Who first added salt to caramel and chocolate and made it a must-have in every bakery and on every dessert menu? That person should be famous!

Hers was not a home where the mother and the grandmother had much-loved recipes handed down through generations, but rather a home where the expected basic meals were served for Sunday brunch as well as Tuesday night. She often wonders if this is the very reason she so loves popcorn in her ice cream and salted caramel in her hot chocolate.

Jo's White Chocolate Covered Popcorn

Makes 2 quarts

NOTE: If you like lots of chocolate on your popcorn, double or triple the chocolate recipe.

- 8 cups air-popped popcorn
- ¾ tsp. salt
- 2 oz. white baking chocolate, chopped
- 1 tsp. butter

1. Place air-popped popcorn in large bowl and salt.

2. In microwave, melt white baking chocolate and butter; stir until smooth. Pour over popcorn mixture and toss to coat.

3. Spread onto waxed paper. Cool until set. Store in airtight container.

White Chocolate Popcorn

Jo's Chocolate Sauce

Makes 2½ cups

- 1 cup water
- ½ cup sugar
- ½ cup light corn syrup
- ¾ cup unsweetened cocoa powder
- 2 oz. bittersweet/semisweet chocolate, finely chopped

1. In medium saucepan, stir together water, sugar, light corn syrup, and cocoa powder.

2. Bring to a boil over medium heat. Once it's just begun to boil, remove from heat and stir in bittersweet or semisweet chocolate until melted.

NOTE: If you allow chocolate to stand for an hour before serving, chocolate will thicken.

White Chocolate Popcorn

Chocolate Sauce

Salted Caramel Ice Cream Sundae's

Jo's Salted Caramel Ice Cream Sundaes

Assemble the sundaes using Jo's Salted Caramel Ice Cream, Jo's Chocolate Sauce, and Jo's White Chocolate Covered Popcorn. The combination is amazing.

Jo's Salted Caramel Bars

Jo's Salted Caramel Ice Cream
{see recipe on page 160}

Hard Shell Covering
{see recipe on page 120}

Jo's White Chocolate Covered Popcorn
{see recipe on page 150}

Cups for moulds {size depends how many you will make}

Popsicle sticks

1. Spoon Jo's Salted Caramel Ice Cream into moulds and insert Popsicle sticks. Freeze until solid; overnight is best.

2. Remove from moulds and dip ends in Hard Shell Covering; sprinkle on Jo's White Chocolate Coverd Popcorn. Be quick to add the popcorn, as chocolate shell dries very fast. Refreeze to firm if needed.

Step 1.

Step 2.

Step 3.

Jo's Frozen Salted Caramel Hot Chocolate

Makes 2 large mugs

- 1 cup milk
- 1 individual-sized instant hot chocolate package
- ½ cup ice cubes
- 2 large scoops Jo's Salted Caramel Ice Cream, plus extra for garnish

  White/dark chocolate shavings, for garnish

1. In saucepan, mix ½ cup milk with hot chocolate package; heat until dissolved. Let mixture cool.

2. In blender, blend cooled hot chocolate mixture, remaining ½ cup milk, and ice cubes. Blend on high until ice is thoroughly crushed.

3. Add caramel ice cream using pulsing speed to mix slightly, leaving chucks of ice cream.

4. Pour into mugs or glasses, adding an extra dollop of ice cream to garnish. Freeze 20 minutes or so to firm up.

5. Add white or dark chocolate shavings just before serving.

Frozen Salted Caramel Hot Chocolate

Joy x 100

Throughout *Everything Goes with Ice Cream* Koralee has given you so many new ideas, but don't forget: you can take the ingredients from one recipe and use them with any other recipe. I love to set out all of the sprinkles used everywhere in this book and let my guests choose which ones to put in my Frozen Salted Caramel Hot Chocolate. Of course, the red candy flowers are my favorite!

A Cozy Goodnight

{all things snugly & delightfully comfy}

We love comfort in our home, and our pajamas would be rated as one of our top cozy items along with warm socks, blankets, and pillows. When trying to come up with the ultimate ice cream comfort treat, the first thing that came to mind was a satisfying thick and creamy vanilla milkshake. By adding warm, melted mini marshmallows to this shake, pure yummy comfort in a glass has been created.

Embellish Your Own Pillowcases

There is just something endearing about pretty floral pillows. We tend to pile them high in our home. Pillowcases are one of the easiest things to sew, but if you don't want to make your own, you can find oodles of lovely premade pillowcases. To spruce them up a bit, all you need to do is sew on some pretty embellishments: lace, pompom trim, rickrack, buttons, doilies, and other bits and pieces. This is such an easy way to cozy up your home and bed.

Marshmallow Vanilla Milkshakes

Makes 4 cups

- 2 cups mini marshmallows, plus extra pink mini marshmallows for garnish
- 1 cup whole milk
- 3 cups vanilla ice cream
- 1½ tsp. vanilla extract

1. Heat oven to broil

2. Warm mini marshmallows on cookie sheet under broiler until just insides are melty. Watch carefully not to brown them; this only takes a few seconds. You want marshmallow centers to be very soft and warm, but outside to look the same. When they puff up, they are ready.

3. Blend whole milk, vanilla ice cream, and vanilla extract in blender.

4. Once completely blended, add melted marshmallows and continue to blend until little pieces of marshmallow are left.

5. Pour shake into cup or refrigerated Dottie Glasses and garnish with pink marshmallows.

you can't buy happiness but you can buy ice cream... and that's kind of the same thing
unknown

Dottie Glasses

For a pretty presentation, serve your milkshakes in a clear glass with marshmallow dots. Just snip mini pink marshmallows in half with scissors and press the cut side against the inside of the glass. Refrigerate glasses for a few minutes before pouring the shake into the dottie glasses. Larger marshmallows are fun too!

Deep-Fried Ice Cream

Now for some extremely fun comfort food, nothing beats Deep-Fried Ice Cream. Once you break into its hard, crunchy shell, out flows a mound of soft, warm ice cream — pure joy! Plus, just the thought of deep frying ice cream makes you want to smile.

Makes 6 cups

4	cups vanilla ice cream
5	cups cornflakes, crushed
1½	TB. cinnamon
2	eggs
1	TB. whole milk
8	cups oil for deep frying
	Parchment paper

1. Make 6 round balls of vanilla ice cream. Place on baking sheet lined with parchment paper and freeze until firm, at least 1 hour.

2. Mix together cornflakes and cinnamon. In another bowl, beat eggs and whole milk together.

3. Remove ice cream from freezer and quickly roll around cornflake mixture, packing cornflakes into ice cream.

4. Roll ice cream balls in egg mixture then back in cornflake mixture. Return to freezer for another hour.

5. Heat oil in heavy pot until temperature reaches 365°F. Remove ice cream balls from freezer and carefully drop into hot oil, deep frying for only about 20 seconds until outsides are brown. Remove from oil and place on paper towel. Serve immediately.

deep
fried
ice
cream

Pink Marshmallows Madness

It's easy to spruce up any flavour of milkshake by adding a handful of mini marshmallows just before serving. Stir them into the milkshake or let them sit on top as a garnish. Try adding colored marshmallows for extra fun.

Take-Home Ice Cream Kit

I wish I could give each one of you one of these sweet take-home kits with my book. They are so easy to pack up and they make quite an impression.

You can start with any type of container that you want to hold all of the ice cream treasures. A clear container is best for showing off pretty contents.

Add some shredded color paper, then fill with your ice cream treats — just think sundaes, banana splits, or ice cream cones, and build from there. Tie the package up with a pretty bow and give to someone who needs their day sweetened up.

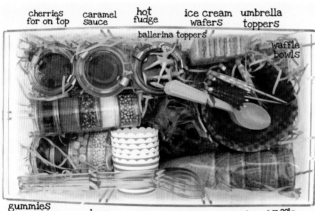

cherries for on top · caramel sauce · hot fudge · ballerina toppers · ice cream wafers · umbrella toppers · waffle bowls

gummies sprinkles candy toppers · long spoons · pretty cups · pretzels · short spoons · waffle cones

sprucing up the vanilla

Conversions & Equivalents

Metric Conversion Chart by Volume (for Liquids)

U.S.	Metric (milliliters/liters)
1/4 teaspoon	1.25 mL
1/2 teaspoon	2.5 mL
1 teaspoon	5 mL
1 tablespoon	15 mL
1/4 cup	60 mL
1/2 cup	120 mL
3/4 cup	180 mL
1 cup	240 mL
2 cups (1 pint)	480 mL
4 cups (1 quart)	960 mL
4 quarts (1 gallon)	3.8 L

Metric Conversion Chart by Weight (for Dry Ingredients)

U.S.	Metric (grams/kilograms)
1/4 teaspoon	1 g
1/2 teaspoon	2 g
1 teaspoon	5 g
1 tablespoon	15 g
16 ounces (1 pound)	450 g
2 pounds	900 g
3 pounds	1.4 kg
4 pounds	1.8 kg
5 pounds	2.3 kg
6 pounds	2.7 kg

Temperature Conversion

Fahrenheit	Celsius	Fahrenheit	Celsius
32º	0º	350º	177º
212º	100º	375º	191º
250º	121º	400º	425º
275º	135º	425º	218º
300º	149º		

WARNING:
Baking in any type of canning jar is not recommend by the manufacturers and is done so at your own risk. Canning jars are designed to withstand hot water sterilization temperatures but run the risk of cracking when placed in a hot dry oven.

Every effort has been made to ensure that all of the information in this book is accurate. However, due to differing conditions, tools, and individual skills, the publisher, author, or contributors cannot be responsible for any injuries, losses, and other damages that may result from the use of the information in this book.

Cooking Measurement Equivalents

3 teaspoons = 1 tablespoon

2 tablespoons = 1 fluid ounce

4 tablespoons = 1/4 cup

5 tablespoons + 1 teaspoon = 1/3 cup

8 tablespoons = 1/2 cup

10 tablespoons + 2 teaspoons = 2/3 cup

12 tablespoons = 3/4 cup

16 tablespoons = 1 cup

48 teaspoons = 1 cup

1 cup = 8 fluid ounces

2 cups = 1 pint

2 pints = 1 quart

4 quarts = 1 gallon

Icing Sugar = Powdered Sugar

Desiccated Coconut = Dried Coconut

Index

mmmm... **got any more?**